T0247800

Life Cycle Management of Military Commercial Derivative Aircraft

Improving FAA Certification, Implementation of Digital Engineering and Sustainment Strategy

BRITTANY CLAYTON, OBAID YOUNOSSI, BRIAN DOLAN,
THOMAS GOUGHNOUR, DEVON HILL, GWEN MAZZOTTA,
BENJAMIN J. SACKS, BARBARA BICKSLER

Prepared for the Department of the Air Force
Approved for public release; distribution is unlimited

PROJECT AIR FORCE

For more information on this publication, visit **www.rand.org/t/RRA1676-2**.

About RAND

The RAND Corporation is a research organization that develops solutions to public policy challenges to help make communities throughout the world safer and more secure, healthier and more prosperous. RAND is nonprofit, nonpartisan, and committed to the public interest. To learn more about RAND, visit www.rand.org.

Research Integrity

Our mission to help improve policy and decisionmaking through research and analysis is enabled through our core values of quality and objectivity and our unwavering commitment to the highest level of integrity and ethical behavior. To help ensure our research and analysis are rigorous, objective, and nonpartisan, we subject our research publications to a robust and exacting quality-assurance process; avoid both the appearance and reality of financial and other conflicts of interest through staff training, project screening, and a policy of mandatory disclosure; and pursue transparency in our research engagements through our commitment to the open publication of our research findings and recommendations, disclosure of the source of funding of published research, and policies to ensure intellectual independence. For more information, visit www.rand.org/about/research-integrity.

RAND's publications do not necessarily reflect the opinions of its research clients and sponsors.

Published by the RAND Corporation, Santa Monica, Calif.
© 2023 RAND Corporation
RAND® is a registered trademark.

Library of Congress Cataloging-in-Publication Data is available for this publication.

ISBN: 978-1-9774-1162-4

Cover: U.S. Air Force photo by Senior Airman Cody Dowell.

Limited Print and Electronic Distribution Rights

This publication and trademark(s) contained herein are protected by law. This representation of RAND intellectual property is provided for noncommercial use only. Unauthorized posting of this publication online is prohibited; linking directly to its webpage on rand.org is encouraged. Permission is required from RAND to reproduce, or reuse in another form, any of its research products for commercial purposes. For information on reprint and reuse permissions, please visit www.rand.org/pubs/permissions.

About This Report

In this report, the authors assess the benefits and challenges of (and propose best practices for) commercial derivative aircraft (CDA) strategies to inform acquisition leadership officials in the U.S. Air Force in case of a future procurement. The authors reviewed existing research related to CDA acquisition to understand the challenges associated with balancing the advantages and disadvantages of pursuing a CDA project. This is a companion report to another 2023 report, *Improving Acquisition and Sustainment Outcomes for Military Commercial Derived Aircraft: The KC-46A* Pegasus *Experience*.

The research reported here was commissioned by the Air Force Life Cycle Management Center and conducted within the Resource Management Program of RAND Project AIR FORCE as part of a fiscal year 2022 project, "Improving Acquisition and Sustainment Outcomes of Commercial Derivative Aircraft."

RAND Project AIR FORCE

RAND Project AIR FORCE (PAF), a division of the RAND Corporation, is the Department of the Air Force's (DAF's) federally funded research and development center for studies and analyses, supporting both the United States Air Force and the United States Space Force. PAF provides the DAF with independent analyses of policy alternatives affecting the development, employment, combat readiness, and support of current and future air, space, and cyber forces. Research is conducted in four programs: Strategy and Doctrine; Force Modernization and Employment; Resource Management; and Workforce, Development, and Health. The research reported here was prepared under contract FA7014-22-D-0001.

Additional information about PAF is available on our website:
www.rand.org/paf/

This report documents work originally shared with the DAF on August 22, 2022. The draft report, dated August 2022, was reviewed by formal peer reviewers and DAF subject-matter experts.

Acknowledgments

We would like to thank Paul Waugh for his contributions to this work. We benefited from helpful action officers, Patrick Shediack and Jacob Gibson, and their teams, who helped facilitate critical meetings and provided meaningful insights. Our research is heavily based on insights provided by a variety of subject matter experts who graciously gave their time. A special thank you to Robert Marx, who was pivotal in providing decades of experience in CDA acquisition. We thank Stephanie Young, director of PAF's Resource Management Program, and Anna Jean

Wirth, associate program director, for their support during this project. We thank John Drew and Greg Sanders for their constructive review of the report.

Summary

Issue

Commercial derivative aircraft (CDA) are aircraft based on a commercial design and modified to accommodate military requirements. The KC-46 is a CDA that pioneered the pursuit of several new and innovative acquisition and sustainment strategies: the employment of digital engineering (DE), the pursuit of Federal Aviation Administration (FAA) certification, and the development and execution of an organically oriented sustainment plan. But the costs and benefits of these strategies for CDA are not well understood. The U.S. Air Force (USAF) asked us to assess the benefits, challenges, and best practices to inform acquisition leadership on the merits of pursuing these strategies for CDA that the USAF might procure in the future.

Approach

To conduct this research, we reviewed existing research related to CDA acquisition to understand the challenges associated with balancing the advantages and disadvantages of pursuing a CDA project; conducted a series of semistructured interviews with the USAF, the FAA, and industry experts; and examined the KC-46A's experience for lessons applicable to future CDA.

Findings

- When considering FAA certification, early, open, and regular communication between all parties can help the Department of the Air Force scope CDA projects and become aware of any issues throughout the process.
- Knowledge and education of FAA certification processes does not appear standardized. This could contribute to confusion or unrealistic expectations of partners.
- When considering the platform's mission and modifications from the base design, we found that more modifications could complicate the FAA certification process.
- Maximizing the overlap of CDA operations with commercial variants and limiting modifications maximizes such benefits as shared parts, infrastructure, and supply chains, which can have important implications for sustainment.
- Although there are many theoretical sustainment benefits cited in existing literature, there is a lack of empirical data demonstrating to what extent the USAF has realized sustainment benefits from a CDA acquisition.
- The expected benefits of a successful CDA program could make the use of DE more difficult, but these risks could be mitigated through early systems engineering and planning efforts.

Recommendations

Our recommendations for the USAF fall into three categories: improving the use of FAA certification, improving the sustainment strategy, and implementing DE concepts.

FAA Certification

- Play a larger role in defining the relationship between all parties in the certification process, beginning with setting realistic internal expectations of what the certification process can provide for the USAF.
- Develop and foster in-house talent for certification and CDA management.
- Conduct consultations with the FAA Military Certification Office before a CDA acquisition decision is made to help the USAF decide on the best course of action and refine requirements. For sustainment, the USAF will need to consider strategies early in the process to take full advantage of the potential benefits of certification. This includes discussions with the FAA about meet-the-intent approvals for maintenance and sustainment of the CDA fleet.

Sustainment

- Invest time and resources in understanding the commercial variant's life cycle prior to and during acquisition to ensure that CDA benefits are maximized and that risks are avoided.
- During acquisition, carefully consider the necessary level of modification required to meet mission objectives and make efforts to minimize modifications when possible if pursuing CDA is the preferred strategy.
- Invest in research and expertise related to the sustainment of CDA, including expertise in Maintenance Steering Group-III maintenance practices and procedures and other commercial best practices.
- Invest in data collection and research to better quantify the potential sustainment benefits of CDA.

Digital Engineering

- Realistically consider all constraints, particularly constraints stemming from the nature of CDA acquisitions. That is, compare benefits and costs against alternative strategy options (DE- and non-DE-based) to ensure that DE is an appropriate and optimal strategy to achieve program goals.
- Realize DE benefits, begin planning DE efforts when forming an acquisition strategy, and begin the planning process by considering priority goals of the program and matching to promising DE activities.
- Apply systems engineering methods to identify DE activities, enablers, and investments required for success.
- Consider equities, responsibilities, and capabilities of partners and stakeholders during planning and the decision to pursue a given DE effort.
- Be wary of following U.S. Department of Defense policy and guidance on DE without considering unique characteristics of a CDA acquisition.

Contents

Figures and Tables

Figures

Tables

Chapter 1. Introduction

Commercial derivative aircraft (CDA) are aircraft based on a commercial design and modified to accommodate military requirements. These platforms start from an existing or modified commercial design and incorporate systems required to accommodate a national security need. Examples of heavily modified CDA include the Air Force's KC-46A *Pegasus* and KC-10 *Extender* and the Navy's P-8 *Poseidon*. The missions of CDA vary from personnel transport to intelligence, surveillance, and reconnaissance to aerial refueling, to name a few. The decision to invest in a CDA program is one that should be and is carefully considered. Although there are benefits of a CDA acquisition, ineffective execution of such programs can inhibit the realization of these benefits.

The KC-46 is the commercial derivative military aircraft that pioneered the pursuit of various new and innovative acquisition and sustainment strategies to include the employment of some digital engineering (DE) approaches during the aircraft's development; the pursuit of Federal Aviation Administration (FAA) certification to take advantage of commercial aircraft updates and obtain access to new and refurbished parts for the aircraft through the global 767 aircraft commercial parts pool; and the development and execution of an organically oriented support plan.

With the adoption of these approaches, the U.S. Air Force (USAF) is anticipating several benefits, including long-term cost savings and greater access to parts needed to operate and support the platform. At the same time, there could be unanticipated cost, schedule, and other impacts associated with pursuing these strategies. The costs and benefits of these strategies for commercial derivative military aircraft are not well understood. As a result, the USAF asked RAND Project AIR FORCE to assess the benefits, challenges, and best practices to inform acquisition leadership on the merits of pursuing these strategies for CDA that the USAF could procure in the future.

Benefits and Challenges of CDA

CDA have several features that can benefit the USAF. These benefits are appealing because they can help reduce development time, manage cost overruns, and reduce risk throughout the acquisition process. A CDA is not a clean sheet design; rather, it leverages an existing commercial design. However, the level of modification for each CDA varies substantially as the examples in Figure 1.1 illustrate.

1

Figure 1.1. Notional Comparison of Various Air Force CDAs Mission Complexity and Level of Modification

This approach assumes reduced development time and allows the USAF to achieve a faster construction start. In a traditional defense aircraft program, the entire aircraft must be designed from scratch, whereas a CDA program incorporates "green" design components that are presumably proven and operable. [1] The only components that need to be newly designed are the militarized systems and touchpoints between those and the green systems.

Another benefit to CDA acquisition is that the lead unit of the CDA program starts far down the production learning curve. As a result, the USAF program can enter the production line after a significant number of units have already been built, enabling it to leverage the efficiencies gained during the first units' construction and assembly. Presumably, this should save cost and reduce the schedule for the CDA program. In addition to leveraging production line efficiencies, CDA can also benefit from other existing processes and infrastructure, such as supply chain, logistics processes, and maintenance facilities. This lessens the burden on the USAF of creating and streamlining these processes themselves.

But for the USAF to realize these benefits, the program must be carefully managed. To start, more benefits can be realized if the system is as green as possible. As with many acquisition programs, requirements for CDA programs tend to expand over the course of the acquisition

---

[1] In this context, *green* refers to the unmodified portion of the commercial design. A CDA that is largely unmodified from the commercial variant is considered green.

program. The further the CDA design deviates from the commercial design, the more expensive and riskier the acquisition becomes.[2]

The USAF also needs to be mindful of the commercial variant's expected retirement. The sundown of the commercial variant can indicate the closure of maintenance and logistics facilities used to sustain it. If the USAF variant leverages these facilities, it might need to find other ways to replace these capabilities. Because the USAF typically flies its aircraft much longer than its commercial counterparts, the end of production for a commercial design is likely to be earlier than that of the military design, which could create a gap in operating capacity for the remaining USAF aircraft. Commercial aircraft retirement could also affect the accessibility of replacement parts if commercial supply lines shutter as systems are removed from use.

Because the USAF does not pay for the development of the commercial design elements of the CDA, obtaining the data rights to these components can be difficult. In a traditional defense program, the USAF would fund the design of the platform and could therefore negotiate technical data rights up front. This is not the case with CDA. This topic is discussed in more detail in Chapter 4 and the appendix.

Best Practices for CDA Acquisition

In this report, we outline lessons in three specific areas of acquisition and sustainment: the role of FAA certification within the CDA process, possible sustainment arrangements that could be most beneficial to CDA, and the application of DE practices in CDA acquisition.

There are, however, some best practices that span these three areas, as detailed in Table 1.1. These crosscutting practices, which were raised during multiple discussions with subject-matter experts (SMEs), primarily focus on organizational experience and knowledge. Although the USAF routinely procures CDA aircraft, no centralized area of expertise exists within the service to document lessons or collect best practices. Most CDA-specific experience resides in a handful of employees. The USAF could benefit from dedicating resources to centralize this knowledge.

Developing training opportunities for acquisition and sustainment professionals could help those involved in the unique features of a CDA program. One approach is embedding USAF personnel into the FAA to gain experience with and exposure to FAA regulations and processes.

---

[2] USAF, *Commercial Derivative Aircraft (CDA) Acquisition Guide*, November 2009.

Table 1.1. Crosscutting Organizational Level Improvements for CDA Programs

Knowledge Share	Training	Awareness/Integration	Expertise
Establish a center of expertise for CDA acquisition that could be accessed by all program offices	Develop training opportunities for acquisition professionals focused on unique features of CDA acquisition	Colocate members of the program office with the prime contractor to better integrate the government into the integrated product team (IPT)	Identify the appropriate level of expertise in critical acquisition areas
Standardize contract clauses/provisions to minimize rework and reduce source selection time	Embed USAF employees into FAA to gain experience with and exposure to FAA regulations and processes	Increase communication with the operating command and bases to monitor requirements development and operational performance	Include lawyers and contract experts during contract development and negotiations
Establish a market research office to share insights into industry experiences and regulatory changes		Partner with airline or aircraft brokers to better understand their contracts (performance, guarantees, warranties, services, etc.)	Engage sustainment experts during contract negotiations
Collaborate with Navy CDA programs to share lessons learned			Address sustainment specifics during contracting phase

Integrating the CDA project team with other key players would enable cohesion throughout the program. Throughout the course of this study, we heard suggestions from experts that varied from colocating program office employees with the prime contractor to partnering with commercial airline brokers. It was also suggested that increasing communication with the sustainment community, specifically operating commands and bases, could be helpful during requirements development.

A critical time in an acquisition's life cycle is during contract negotiations. Having the appropriate expertise available during negotiations is essential to a comprehensive and successful contract. Needed expertise includes lawyers, those with specific knowledge of CDA acquisition, sustainment experts, and others. Identifying critical data rights and sustainment specifics early will help set the program up for success throughout the life of the platform.

Objective and Approach

Our examination of strategies for procuring and sustaining CDA focused on the following research questions:

- What is the best use of FAA certification for CDA acquisition?
- What are the best uses of organic and contractor logistics support (CLS) arrangements for CDA sustainment?
- How can the USAF bring design into the digital space and use that to benefit the acquisition life cycle of CDA?

- What lessons learned can we leverage from the KC-46 experience in these areas?

To answer these questions, we took a multimethod approach. First, we reviewed existing research surrounding CDA acquisition. Several reports have been published about the uniqueness of CDA programs, which provided a solid foundation for understanding the challenge that the USAF will face in balancing the advantages and disadvantages of pursuing a CDA project. Second, we conducted discussions with a variety of SMEs. We identified several organizations that play a role in the acquisition of CDA platforms and held a series of meetings to learn about their perspectives on CDA acquisition. These organizations included the following:

- Air Force Cost Analysis Agency
- Air Force Life Cycle Management Center/Mobility & Training Aircraft Directorate (AFLCMC/WL)
- Air Force Sustainment Center (AFSC)
- European Union Aviation Safety Agency (EASA)
- FAA Military Certification Office (MCO)
- Georgia Technical Research Institute
- KC-46 Program Office
- KC-46 Sustainment SMEs
- Presidential & Executive Airlift Directorate
- Office of the Secretary of the Air Force, Acquisition, Technology, & Logistics.

We documented these discussions and consolidated recurring themes offered in each. Finally, we conducted a series of roundtable discussions that focused on key findings and recommendations. These discussions created a space for SMEs to discuss our findings and recommendations in detail and provide additional insights, corrections, and edits.

Organization of This Report

This report is organized into five chapters, followed by one appendix. In Chapter 2, we describe the role of the FAA within CDA acquisition and highlight some best practices. In Chapter 3, we discuss the spectrum of sustainment arrangements and those best suited for CDA platforms. In Chapter 4, we explore DE practices for CDA acquisition and highlight specific challenges with implementation. The report concludes in Chapter 5 with a summary of key observations and recommendations. The appendix provides a summary of some recent RAND Corporation work related to technical data rights and intellectual property (IP).

In a companion to this report, *Improving Acquisition and Sustainment Outcomes for Military Commercial Derived Aircraft: The KC-46A* Pegasus *Experience*, we documented the KC-46A experience.[3] This supplemental report summarizes KC-46A acquisition in the three focus areas

---

[3] Benjamin J. Sacks, Obaid Younossi, and Brittany Clayton, *Improving Acquisition and Sustainment Outcomes for Military Commercial Derived Aircraft: The KC-46A* Pegasus *Experience*, RAND Corporation, RR-A1676-1, 2023.

we cover in this report: the use of FAA certification, the plan for sustainment arrangements, and the role of DE in the acquisition process.

Chapter 2. The Role of FAA Certification in CDA Acquisition

Department of the Air Force (DAF) policy requires military CDA to achieve and maintain FAA certification to the maximum extent practical. Indeed, for the KC-46A, the USAF sought FAA certification to a greater extent than on any previous heavily modified military CDA. This process, intended to provide various benefits, is a complex one that might not always achieve the desired outcomes for several reasons.

RAND was asked to review and assess the USAF's use of the FAA certification processes for military CDA. To guide our research and analysis, and to suggest ways that could improve the USAF's experience with the process, we sought to answer the following questions:

- What is the theoretical case for pursuing FAA certification for military CDA? Does this case bear out in practice?
- Where might there be challenges with current FAA certification processes for military CDA? Where are opportunities for improvement?
- Under which circumstances can FAA certification provide added value for a CDA acquisition program?

To answer these questions, we reviewed DAF policy, FAA regulations, and other literature to understand the CDA certification process and historical context. We also spoke with several SMEs from the USAF, the FAA MCO, and EASA, who were invaluable in providing further insights and sharing their knowledge to better understand possible challenges and shortcomings in the military CDA certification process.

In the following sections, we provide background on FAA aircraft certification, lay out the argument for certification of military CDA, share lessons from the EASA experiences, and discuss challenges to military CDA certification. We conclude with considerations that could improve the USAF experience of obtaining and maintaining FAA certification to the maximum extent possible.

Background to FAA Certification for Military CDA

The FAA is responsible for certifying civil aircraft and parts to ensure they are designed, manufactured, tested, and maintained in accordance with (IAW) prescribed safety standards.[4] It does this via three main certification processes:

- **FAA Type Certifications (TCs), Amended TCs (ATCs), or Supplemental TCs (STCs)** serve as approval that the design of the aircraft and its component parts (e.g.,

---

[4] See U.S. Code, Title 49, Transportation, Subtitle VII, Aviation Programs, Part A, Subpart III, Safety, Chapter 447, Safety Regulation, Section 44701, General Requirements.

engines, control stations, propellers) meet civil aviation regulatory requirements for safe operation.

- **FAA Production Certification** is a determination that an aircraft manufacturer is able to consistently assemble products under FAA-approved TC designs and has effective quality assurance and manufacturing inspection systems in place.
- **Airworthiness Certification** is official authorization for the operation of a certified aircraft. This signifies that the aircraft has been manufactured in conformance with the issued TC design, is operated and maintained within approved limits, that any alterations are made IAW FAA-approved practices, that Airworthiness Directives are complied with, and that supporting documentation meets FAA standards. This is required for individual aircraft that must be registered with the FAA and display the assigned N-number.[5]

Even for civil passenger aircraft, achieving certification is a complicated, multiphase process that can take anywhere from five to nine years for a new aircraft type design, or three to five years for an ATC.[6] Timely completion of a successful commercial certification process depends on various interlinked factors, such as the following:

- mutual trust between the FAA and applicant (the aircraft manufacturer)
- commitments to confidentiality
- agreements to meet responsibilities
- open and timely communication
- early and well-documented familiarization meetings
- ongoing meetings with all key players in attendance
- agreement on time frames and expectations
- production of high-quality documentation of decisions and agreements
- adherence to other expectations outlined in guidance.[7]

The FAA works closely with the civil aviation industry to ensure compliance with safety standards. To that end, the FAA and industry periodically publish an industry guide to product certification. Certification statutes, regulations, rules, and FAA orders are publicly available but this guide is a collective effort to "lay a foundation from which to build mutual trust, leadership, teamwork, efficient business practices, and maturing Applicant certification competencies."[8] No such jointly coauthored guidebook appears to exist between FAA and the military services, though the U.S. Department of Defense (DoD) and the DAF do have their own separate

---

[5] William Stockman, Milt Ross, Robert Bongiovi, and Greg Sparks, *Successful Integration of Commercial Systems: A Study of Commercial Derivative Systems*, PESystems, Inc. and Dayton Aerospace, Inc., 2011; Federal Aviation Administration, "Certification," webpage, June 17, 2022; and U.S. Code, Title 49, Transportation, Subtitle VII, Aviation Programs, Part A, Subpart III, Safety, Chapter 447, Safety Regulation, Section 44704 (b), Supplemental Type Certificates.

[6] Federal Aviation Administration, "Airworthiness Certification," webpage, June 29, 2022.

[7] Aerospace Industries Association, Aircraft Electronics Association, General Aviation Manufacturers Association, and Federal Aviation Administration, *The FAA and Industry Guide to Product Certification*, 3rd ed., May 2017.

[8] Aerospace Industries Association et al., 2017, p. 1.

certification guidance for CDA programs. The industry guide provides less technical, more straightforward direction while laying out roles and responsibilities of key partners.

Ensuring Safety

As the United States' civil aviation authority, the FAA's highest priority is the safety of passengers. Its mission is "to provide the safest, most efficient aerospace system in the world," further underscored by a values statement that starts with, "Safety is our passion."[9] Although this is ideal for ensuring the well-being of passengers and public confidence in air travel, military CDA projects can be more nuanced. The FAA's review of the KC-46A, for instance, primarily considered safety. Consider, for example, the KC-46A's procedure that requires it to connect to another aircraft to transfer fuel, either through the centerline boom or the centerline or wing hose-and-drogue systems. This connection, regularly used in military missions, has no comparable civilian procedure. The FAA will, of course, want to be sure the necessary components do not pose a risk to the aircraft.[10]

The Technical Airworthiness Authority (TAA) places a high premium on the safety of military aircraft and the personnel who fly them but has a different risk tolerance to ensure that an aircraft performs to specification. There is also a USAF management process that allows for acceptance of certain risk if thoroughly explained and approved by the appropriate official.[11]

Military Certification Office Branch

The FAA's MCO branch was established in 2005 to oversee military CDA certification projects and to guide service personnel through the process while ensuring proper integration with regulations.[12] This branch serves to smooth the process for military sponsors but does not alleviate all challenges, which we discuss later in this chapter. It should also be noted that certain military equipment is outside the scope of FAA's expertise and ineligible for certification, specifically

- combat systems, whether defensive or offensive
- gun, missile, and bombing systems
- electronic jamming systems
- tow targets
- military organic aircraft
- certain military systems or components that might require a special condition or exemption or are unique only to a military or special mission function

---

[9] Federal Aviation Administration, "Mission," webpage, undated.

[10] Test and Evaluation SMEs, interview with the authors, June 28, 2022.

[11] See Department of the Air Force, "Risk Identification and Acceptance for Airworthiness Determinations," Headquarters Aeronautical Systems Center (AFMC), Wright-Patterson Air Force Base, Bulletin AWB-013A, June 29, 2011.

[12] FAA MCO SMEs, interview with the authors, January 5, 2022.

- any installed systems that could pose a hazard to the aircraft, nearby aircraft, or personnel or property while the aircraft is on the ground or in flight.[13]

Usually, these systems require an explanation of their intended operation and separate approval by military authorities.

The Case for Military CDA

The case for military CDA largely rests on assumptions that they will cost less to modify, purchase, and sustain than typical military aircraft.[14] Here, we discuss the impetus for military CDA and the feasibility of achieving potential benefits. We note that we use the terms *original equipment manufacturer* (OEM), *contractor*, and *applicant* interchangeably throughout the remainder of this chapter. They all refer to the same party in this process: the aircraft manufacturer selected by the USAF to make modifications to a selected base-certified commercial aircraft and prove compliance with FAA regulations.

Policy and Regulatory Impetus

Multiple DAF policy statements or guidance documents state that, in some shape or form, the service branch shall

> Obtain and maintain Federal Aviation Administration type certification for civil aircraft acquired or modified by the Air Force if the primary mission for the aircraft is the transport of passengers. For all other civil aircraft acquired or modified by the Air Force, the Air Force shall obtain and maintain Federal Aviation Administration type certification to the maximum extent practical.[15]

DAF policy requires achievement of FAA certification to the "maximum extent practical" to reduce the costs and development time of an aircraft program and as part of a trend within the military services to maximize the use of commercial-off-the-shelf items.

USAF and FAA Certification Processes

As mentioned previously, the FAA and the USAF have slightly different safety and risk tolerances. Whereas the FAA prioritizes the safety of the aircraft and its passengers above *all* other concerns, the USAF, while also prioritizing safety, has some tolerance for risk to optimize

---

[13] Federal Aviation Administration Order 8110.101A, *Type Certification Procedures for Military Commercial Derivative Aircraft*, Federal Aviation Administration, February 25, 2015.

[14] Stockman et al., 2011, pp. 24–30.

[15] Air Force Policy Directive 62-6, *USAF Airworthiness*, Department of the Air Force, January 16, 2019. See also Air Force Instruction 62-601, *USAF Airworthiness*, Department of the Air Force, June 11, 2010; and DoD, *Department of Defense Handbook: Airworthiness Certification Criteria*, MIL-HDBK-516C, December 12, 2014.

operational performance or mission success. There is a "safety release valve" process that allows for one-off acceptance of higher risks if approved by the appropriate USAF authorities.[16]

CDA are required to maintain FAA certification for the life of the aircraft.[17] This is the case for the KC-46A. One study on the integration of military CDA notes that if the USAF operates and maintains aircraft under full FAA certification, airworthiness, and civil registration throughout its life, then the FAA considers the USAF an owner-operator under its guidelines as if it were any other civilian carrier. That study indicated there are few USAF examples in this category, naming Aero Club aircraft or leased personnel transport aircraft as examples.[18] To maintain FAA TC of a CDA acquired and operated by DoD, a military service must take action to ensure compliance with FAA oversight, namely complying with rules concerning operation, maintenance, repair, documentation, and reporting.[19]

For military CDA, the USAF heavily leverages the FAA TC, essentially transferring the civilian certification to the military certification. The normal military process requires the TAA to establish, approve, and maintain airworthiness for each fleet type. That is, the TAA verifies the ability of an aircraft design to fly safely and then issues a military type certificate (MTC) that provides evidence that the aircraft's design complies with rules and regulations. After this, the program manager for the aircraft issues a military certificate of airworthiness to each individual aircraft that proves compliance with the MTC and can be safely operated.[20] At the time of this report's writing, the KC-46A had received its ATC, STC, and was awaiting its MTC pending resolution of the remote vision system deficiencies and FAA certification of its wing aerial refueling pods.

Maintenance and sustainment, which are discussed in more detail in Chapter 3, also factor into the certification process. Part of maintaining FAA TC involves maintaining approved aircraft in compliance with FAA rules. This will be the case for the KC-46A. However, the USAF does not follow an FAA-approved maintenance program, nor does the FAA approve USAF repair facilities. Review of FAA and USAF regulations can allow for meet-the-intent (MTI) approval of USAF regulations to maintain FAA-approved type design, TC, and airworthiness certification to the greatest extent possible.[21]

The KC-46 received two such MTI approvals, one for AFSC military repair state depot and another for organizational-level maintenance. According to the Defense Acquisition University, the KC-46A's MTI effort is "easily adaptable/scalable to other military CDA programs as a

---

[16] USAF SME, interview with the authors, May 26, 2022; See also Department of the Air Force, 2011.

[17] Air Force Policy Directive 62-6, 2019.

[18] Stockman et al., 2011, p. 49.

[19] Stockman et al., 2011, p. 50.

[20] Air Force Policy Directive 62-6, 2019; Stockman et al., 2011, p. 51.

[21] For more information on MTI, see Defense Acquisition University, "Military Commercial Derivative Aircraft (MCDA) and Federal Aviation Administration (FAA) Approved Meet the Intent (MTI)," webpage, undated-b.

baseline for an effort to recognize the platform as MTI and gain FAA concurrence." Because there is no overarching MTI framework, other platforms would need to seek individual FAA MTI approval.[22]

Part of the planning stages for a new program and early discussions between the USAF sponsoring office and the FAA MCO should be clearly defining the civil and military airworthiness seams. According to 2009 CDA acquisition guidance, military CDA projects are best thought of as hybrid certification projects because the FAA certifies type design changes, and the military approves some modifications.[23] The more modified an aircraft is from its FAA-certified base commercial design, the more its airworthiness and certification will depend on military processes. This seam requires the USAF to coordinate with the OEM to ensure all aspects of the CDA certification flow between civil and military processes. In Figure 2.1, the red line shows the airworthiness junction. Items above the red line are processes that the FAA approves and items below the red line are processes that the USAF approves.

Figure 2.1. FAA and Military Certification Seam

Level of FAA Approval	Aspect Approved by FAA or USAF			
Full Approval	Equipment Qualification	Installation Approval	No Restrictions on Use	STC
Limited Approval	Equipment Qualification	Installation Approval	Military Use Only With	STC
			Statement of Functionality	
Safe Carriage	Equipment Qualification*	Installed; Not Connected	Operational Approval	STC/MTC
	Equipment Qualification	Connected for Operation		
Provisions Only	Equipment Qualification	Installation Approval	Operational Approval	STC/MTC
None	Equipment Qualification	Installation Approval	Operational Approval	MTC

SOURCE: Adapted from United States Air Force Airworthiness Bulletin (AWB)-360, *Commercial Derivative Aircraft Airworthiness*, Department of the Air Force, September 1, 2021.
NOTE: The red line shows the airworthiness junction. Items above the red line are processes that the FAA approves and items below the red line are processes that the USAF approves.
* For FAA equipment qualification in a nonfunctional state, additional testing may be required.

It is the responsibility of the OEM to qualify or demonstrate compliance with the USAF's TAA standards. For certification and airworthiness approvals that fall outside the FAA's typical authority, the FAA MCO cannot require the OEM to provide documentation proving compliance with hazard and system safety assessments that encompass USAF-approved modifications; that

---

[22] Defense Acquisition University, undated-b.

[23] USAF, 2009.

responsibility belongs to the USAF and the OEM.[24] In short, when managing a new military CDA program, it is the responsibility of the USAF to determine the seams between civil and military certification/airworthiness processes, ensure that the OEM understands these definitions and adheres to them in a timely manner, and ensure that regular communication occurs between all parties to prevent confusion and to help anticipate challenges.

The ideal successful military CDA project is one that delivers as many of the anticipated benefits to the USAF as possible while both minimizing cost overruns and scheduling delays and ensuring that all stakeholders are satisfied with the outcome. FAA- and civil aviation industry–authored certification guidance outlines the roles and responsibilities of key players. It also emphasizes the importance of relationships by using words and phrases such as *teamwork*, *open and frequent communication*, *issue resolution processes*, *mutual trust*, and *mutually agreed upon commitments*.[25] Separate USAF and FAA guidance for military CDA programs outline roles and responsibilities of key players. A summarized breakdown from the more detailed FAA certification guidance for military CDA programs is included in Figure 2.2.

---

[24] USAF, 2009.

[25] USAF, 2009.

Figure 2.2. FAA Order 8110 Roles and Responsibilities

Military Certification Office (MCO)	Military Aviation Authority (MAA)	Applicant
• Assess scope of the project and determine if the applicant's proposed certification strategies are viable and feasible • Evaluate the applicant's proposed certification plan • Manage and coordinate projects (Order 8110.4 and 8110.101A) • Coordinate with CDA PM to determine whether a PSSA is needed • Help prepare PSSA SOW, to include detailed workload and cost estimates • Help the ACO with problems unique to CDA • Communicate policy and guidance needs • Serve as focal point for any technical issues • Seek help from experts as needed • Serve as POC for ACO program manager or engineer • Coordinate through MAA and respond to questions • Coordinate with MAA on any aspects of the design that are not FAA-approved • Coordinate issue papers between the applicant, MCO, and accountable directorate • Participate in military program meetings when invited	• Understand rules and policy governing the relationship between the applicant and FAA • Understand applicant's rights and responsibilities when pursuing FAA approval under civil regulations • Work together with the MCO to define airworthiness requirements for MCDA • Invite FAA to participate as a consultant on FAA regulations and procedures • Ask FAA to present its views on specific issues, or to provide general project status from its perspective	• Demonstrate the product meets minimum safety standards • Conduct project according to Order 8110.4 • Submit a project specific certification plan (PSCP) providing an approach for showing compliance • Include proposed use of authorized FAA-delegated organization, company designees, and/or qualified outside designees in project • Cover unique aspects to the CDA modifications • Inform MCO and MAA of modifications that are not part of the proposed type design (not FAA-approved) • Identify any known or potential certification or qualification problems early in the process • Clearly identify content and intent of the STC approval in relationship to other modifications that may be made to the aircraft • Indicate if military participation in FAA technical coordination or official board meetings is permissible. Applicant has the right to conduct business and discussion with the FAA in private • Comply with the requirements for continued airworthiness for the TC

SOURCE: Adapted from Federal Aviation Administration Order 8110.101A, 2015.
NOTES: ACO = Aircraft Certification Office; PM = program manager; POC = point of contact; PSSA = Preliminary System Safety Assessment; SOW = statement of work.

Potential Benefits

Pursuance of certification for CDA is generally expected to yield various benefits for the USAF. In the case of the KC-46A, potential advantages include access to the global parts pool, use of precertified components, competition for parts development and sustainment, and avoidance of "vendor lock" over IP rights. Vendor lock is a situation where a customer—in this case the USAF—is wholly dependent on a single vendor, the aircraft OEM, for proprietary items over the lifetime of the purchased equipment and is unable to transition to a different source without significant costs.

U.S. law does provide DoD with unlimited rights to technical data that relate to the form, fit, or function (FFF) of an acquired item or is necessary for its operation, maintenance, installation, or training (OMIT).[26] FAA certification further requires the OEM to provide additional flight worthiness data to commercial operators for collective use, including by third parties, but does not define the term *flight worthiness data*.[27]

Breaking vendor lock has some sustainment implications, including allowing for more competition, which are discussed more fully in Chapter 3 and the KC-46A supplemental case study report.[28] The OEM does, however, retain considerable control over data not in the categories discussed. Indeed, because OMIT data are not clearly defined, Boeing and the USAF are currently in court wrangling over that definition and how much data Boeing should hand over to the USAF.

Further theoretical benefits include a potential reduction of the USAF's flight test program. This benefit occurs because TAAs can accept the results of testing and verification already performed by the FAA, avoiding duplication of some processes. There is also the potential to reduce the amount of data required during the development process because those data already exist or have been supplied at the time to initial operational capability (IOC). In short, leveraging FAA certification for CDA will ideally speed up the development and acquisition of an aircraft.

It is important to note that these are *potential* benefits of pursuing FAA certification. One SME suggested that for the USAF to fully reap the benefits of military CDA, programs would need a standardized "business approach" instead of being allowed to find their own paths to tailoring acquisition processes.[29] Some benefits, such as the potentially shortened time to IOC, are only likely to be realized with rigorous planning and cooperation between the USAF, OEM, and the FAA MCO. In the case of the KC-46A, one representative noted that there had been some benefit to the program in the development and production efforts in part because FAA's expertise and unfettered access to OEM information helped.[30] However, OEM mistakes and overly ambitious schedules set FAA certifications and IOC back by several years.

Potential Pitfalls

There are potential difficulties and other points of consideration that might make pursuing FAA certification less desirable in some instances. As discussed in Chapter 1, advantages are

---

[26] See U.S. Code, Title 10, Armed Forces, Subtitle A, General Military Law, Part V, Acquisition, Subpart D, General Contracting Provisions, Chapter 275, Proprietary Contractor Data and Rights in Technical Data, Subchapter I, Rights in Technical Data, Section 3771, Rights in Technical Data: Regulations.

[27] Richard Van Atta, Royce Kneece, Michael Lippitz, and Christina Patterson, *Department of Defense Access to Intellectual Property for Weapons Systems Sustainment*, Institute for Defense Analyses, IDA Paper P-8266, May 2017, p. 38; and Frank Camm, Philip Carter, Sheng Tao Li, and Melissa Shostak, *Managing Intellectual Property Relevant to Operating and Sustaining Major U.S. Air Force Weapons Systems*, RAND Corporation, RR-4252-AF, 2021, p. 6.

[28] Sacks, Younossi, and Clayton, 2023.

[29] USAF SME, interview with the authors, November 19, 2021.

[30] USAF SME, interview with the authors, January 10, 2022.

optimized when a CDA is as close to its commercial variant as possible. That is, the CDA is unmodified or as green as possible and has a similar mission profile to its civil design. It might be simpler to modify a commercial passenger aircraft for use as a military transport, for example, than to modify one for use in a purely military mission. More-complex missions or modifications can reduce potential benefits or increase development time and acquisition and sustainment costs.

On the issue of the global parts pool, the USAF can more easily draw from the pool than contribute to it. This is in part because of the lack of FAA-approved maintenance depots that we previously discussed. One SME noted that the USAF can return parts to the commercial marketplace if they go through an FAA-certified facility, which is not always practical.[31] That SME did not elaborate on the reasons why, but others implied that impracticalities might include traceability of parts from the manufacturer. The USAF does not order or track parts the same way that the commercial industry does, and once a spare part is repaired at a USAF depot, it has to stay within the USAF supply chain.[32] Furthermore, civil aviation industry skepticism of the reuse of military parts limits the USAF's ability to contribute to the parts pool. Because the USAF can still pull from the parts pool, difficulties in contributing to the parts pool is likely not a major factor when considering pursuance of FAA certification. The use of used civilian Boeing 767 parts was certainly a consideration in choosing the FAA to certify the KC-46A.

It is also important to note that certification for any TC is a complex, multistep process. Even though a CDA starts from a prior FAA-certified design, new engineering or safety concerns might arise and must be satisfied before the FAA MCO is able to sign off on a modified design. Components and other parts that were certified as pieces of one design will not be automatically approved if included in the design of a modified military CDA.

Furthermore, the OEM sets the schedule for the FAA certification processes as part of its certification plan. As was the case with the KC-46A, ambitious assumptions in that timeline can lead to unrealistic expectations among stakeholders, including the USAF as the military sponsor. Unrealistic assumptions are likely to lead to disappointment, especially when timeline slippages occur during the certification process. Further challenges are discussed later in this report.

Conditions of a Successful Program

Based on a review and discussion of the guidance with SMEs, the FAA certification process is not itself an issue. However, the KC-46A supplemental report details how relationship management, expectations, misunderstandings, and a lack of communication can hinder that process. As the sponsor and funder of military CDA projects, the USAF should take responsibility for ensuring all parties are involved in or made aware of key decisions by building mutual trust and providing for open, ongoing communications between all three parties. FAA

---

[31] USAF SME, interview with the authors, November 19, 2021.

[32] USAF SMEs, interview with the authors, February 7, 2022.

SMEs used the analogy of a three-legged stool to illustrate the necessity of all parties carrying their weight equally; one weak leg can unbalance the entire situation.[33] Based on our research, conditions of a successful military CDA project include

- knowledge and understanding of the FAA certification process
- knowledge and understanding of USAF guidance
- early discussions between the USAF and FAA
- regular, open, and ongoing communications between all parties once the OEM is selected
- mutual understanding of roles, responsibilities, and commitments
- mutual agreement to certification timelines
- mutual trust
- CDA with as few modifications as possible
- avoidance of requirements creep as the CDA is certified.

Lessons from the European Union Aviation Safety Agency

The practice of using CDA for military purposes is not unique to the United States. Through our research, we learned how the CDA certification process works in the European Union (EU), and EASA's role in certification of CDA for military purposes by its member states.[34] Established in 2002, EASA is the civil aviation agency of the EU. The certification process for a military CDA involves several parties, including EASA; the Organisation for Joint Armament Co-Operation (OCCAR), a European intergovernmental agency with its own certification entity known as the Certification and Qualification Committee (CQC) that approves certain military aircraft; national military authorities for the member state; and the manufacturer of the CDA (for example, Airbus, as in the case of the A330 MRTT tanker aircraft).[35]

EASA member states choose to pursue civil certification of military CDA for similar reasons as U.S. defense organizations. These benefits include access to the global parts pool and depot maintenance and maximizing the use of an exceptional civil safety standard. Some components or systems of the aircraft, however, do not meet the high standard of safety of civil regulations and therefore cannot be certified civilly. Military entities of EASA member-states might value the operational performance derived from them and will defer to certifying those components to military airworthiness. This practice occurs in the United States as well.

Similar to the CDA airworthiness seam previously discussed for U.S. certification projects, there is a seam or "interface" within European practices for CDA where EASA stops certifying

---

[33] FAA SME, interview with the authors, January 5, 2022.

[34] EASA is an agency of the EU that focuses on aviation safety, with main duties related to aviation rulemaking and implementation; safety and environmental certification of aircraft, parts, and engines; inspections; training; and standardization of rules across all national aviation authorities of its 31 member states (27 EU member states plus four partners). The agency also provides technical expertise to national aviation authorities where needed, among other responsibilities. European Union Aviation Safety Agency, "About EASA," webpage, undated.

[35] EASA SME, interview with the authors, May 31, 2022.

to its standards and the OCCAR begins its certification.[36] Much of the discussion among the entities involved in the process is about this seam because it is difficult to draw precisely and determine the scope of responsibility for each entity. This initial step of identifying the seam is important to understanding how to certify to the maximum extent possible, and often the details are outlined in a document.

For example, we learned from expert discussions that perhaps the military authority would choose a CDA with approximately 80 percent commonality with the commercial version and would focus on certifying the remaining 20 percent. The concept of determining parts of commonality can quickly become convoluted when both hardware and software are intermingled. For example, two very similar flight deck displays might be used in both a commercial aircraft and military variant, but the software of the military version might add functionality that precludes it from being certified civilly. This was not the case for the KC-46A, which used the FAA-certified 767-400 Rockwell Collins glass cockpit.

According to expert insight, even though this is a difficult exercise, once the seam is clearly determined, neither the military nor civil entity interferes with the other's certification process. For what relates to civil certification, the military authority is invited to attend meetings but does not interfere with the civil certification process itself unless EASA reaches a point during the certification process where it cannot certify a component that it originally planned to. This process has resulted in a positive dynamic among all parties.

The relationship between CQC/OCCAR, EASA, and the applicant is similar to the U.S. model, though perhaps with even more transparency. Commercial aircraft vendors have concerns about who industry applicants plan to share proprietary information with. But a positive relationship is still facilitated by taking the time to determine the "interface" of airworthiness processes up front.[37] Regular meetings among the three entities help to keep the lines of communication open even though the military authority does not interfere with the certification process between EASA and the applicant. These regular meetings can also serve as an opportunity for all parties to better understand both the civil and military standards and regulations.

If problems arise during the certification process, they most often appear in the continued airworthiness phase because the issuance of a TC by EASA is not the end of EASA's involvement. Continued airworthiness and monitoring of operations necessitates an ongoing relationship. Analyzing small incidents per regulations can sometimes be difficult, as EASA requires feedback from the end user to ensure continued airworthiness and compliance. This type of oversight role has the potential to create frustrations on both sides, especially because the end user in this case typically does not fall under EASA's oversight.

---

[36] EASA SME, interview with the authors, May 31, 2022.

[37] EASA SME, interview with the authors, May 31, 2022.

EASA strives to capture lessons and carry forward insights from previous experiences of CDA certification to inform the process of the next CDA. EASA has recognized that greener aircraft allows the military to capitalize on commonality to use civil certification to the maximum extent possible. Transparency among the parties has helped to cultivate a positive relationship among EASA, CQC/OCCAR, and the applicant. In addition, taking time to determine the "seam"—at the most granular level possible—and then respecting where that line has been drawn has proven successful for setting expectations and creating clear boundaries of authority and responsibility. Given similar motivations, processes, and challenges that exist in European and U.S. CDA certification processes, the United States might find some practices from the European model useful to employ.

Challenges to the Certification of USAF CDA

Given the baseline understanding of the certification process for military CDA, we discuss potential challenges in more detail. All were noted as potential challenges either in literature, guidance, or discussions with SMEs.

First, the level of modification from the green or original FAA-type certified design can make the path to achieving an ATC/STC more difficult. The FAA will not certify certain equipment, and some modifications will require thorough explanation and perhaps subsequent TAA certification or approval for a military CDA to be approved for operations. For example, the boom for a refueling tanker has no civilian counterpart and is outside of the FAA's typical expertise. This and other military-use equipment must be considered, explained, approved, and tested separately from other parts of the aircraft design that are certified IAW the safety standards. To lessen the challenge, it is incumbent on all parties—especially the USAF—to be transparent about system requirements and to engage in open dialogue at the earliest stages of the process. The KC-46A tested Boeing, the USAF, and the FAA in certifying a CDA that had undergone significant changes from the 767-400.

The FAA's position as a regulatory agency that ensures and approves compliance should be understood. The certification process is a relationship between the OEM/applicant and the FAA. The USAF has a role to play as the sponsoring agency for military CDA, but it is the OEM that must prove compliance to the FAA. Any data or proprietary information passed between the OEM and FAA cannot be shared with other agencies, including the sponsoring agency that will eventually acquire the CDA. Any information that the USAF needs access to for the life cycle of the procured CDA should be outlined early and negotiated as part of the contracting process, not after or during the certification process. Furthermore, according to MCO SMEs, the FAA can make recommendations during the process but cannot compel parties. Although the OEM and applicant are entitled to a TC upon application, they must still prove compliance with FAA standards. The FAA can recommend actions to come into compliance, but it is up to the OEM to accept recommendations and make modifications.[38] In this event, the USAF should be involved in discussions regarding difficulties and discourage the OEM to attempt to bypass FAA procedures by seeking military approval.

Another potential challenge to certification is the need to adhere to the program schedule. As part of its certification plan, the OEM is responsible for proposing a feasible schedule that recognizes the scope and magnitude of the certification process.[39] Although the FAA might reject a certification plan if the schedule does not provide adequate understanding of the scope of the project, it is incumbent on the OEM to meet milestones in that plan. Any slippages in reaching milestone dates could result in a delay in final certification. When sponsoring a military CDA program, the USAF should consider if the proposed schedule anticipates delays in the event of any problems during the implementation and testing phases. In the case of the KC-46A, Boeing's accelerated schedule for FAA and military certification proved to be too ambitious for the OEM.

Because the certification process focuses on the FAA and the OEM/applicant, the USAF's insight might be limited. This could cause certain problems such as delays in description of systems designed for military-specific missions and explanations of TAA approval for certain items. According to FAA Order 8110.101A, the OEM can indicate when military participation in FAA coordination or board meetings is permissible, noting that the OEM/applicant has the right to conduct business and discussions in private.[40] The USAF, in establishing its relationship with the OEM and through its contract, might have opportunities to be more prescriptive in ensuring its inclusion/participation in processes.

USAF SMEs indicated a lack of a centralized knowledge base for military CDA programs and FAA certification processes within the service. In addition, there is little or no training for USAF personnel on CDA programs and FAA certification processes. As a result, institutional knowledge is limited and personnel assigned to a new program might have to learn from scratch. According to guidance, the FAA MCO should be consulted very early in the process, and its SMEs appeared eager to be engaged to provide education and help share expertise to shape programs. Some SMEs indicated some frustration with the lack of a defined timeline where outreach to the FAA MCO should take place; others, while not defining a timeline, noted that the relationship between the USAF and the FAA MCO was such that their role as advisers to any program should be sought out and taken advantage of almost from a CDA's program inception before even a base design or OEM is considered.[41] Furthermore, it does not appear that the USAF takes full advantage of the FAA MCO's expertise on an ongoing basis at an point before,

---

[38] MCO SMEs, interviews with the authors, January 5, 2022, and February 1, 2022.

[39] Federal Aviation Administration Order 8110.4C Change 6, *Type Certification*, Federal Aviation Administration, October 12, 2005, change 6, March 6, 2017.

[40] Federal Aviation Administration Order 8110.101A, February 25, 2015.

[41] USAF SME, interview with the authors, August 5, 2022.

during, or after a certification process. Indeed, lessons from prior experiences do not appear to be collected or shared widely within the USAF acquisition complex.

The EASA collects, analyzes, and shares lessons and after-action reports as a best practice within its organization.[42] The AFLCMC's Acquisition Center of Excellence should be able to guide standardized collection of best practices and work-arounds to challenges encountered by CDA programs to allow newer programs to better manage their CDA projects. Finally, the Acquisition Center of Excellence or some other USAF organization could be useful in better engaging the FAA MCO on an ongoing basis to better train personnel on FAA's certification processes. Access to this type of information could enhance enterprise-wide understanding of the certification process, which could help the USAF better leverage its position when drawing up contracts with an OEM, managing relationships, and help avoid disappointment by improving awareness of what FAA certification provides the USAF when properly pursued—including expectation management.

Finally, even a well-managed military CDA program is likely to be subject to cost overruns, scheduling delays, or increases in risk, as the KC-46A experience demonstrated. Although well managed, the program was still subject to component issues and flight-testing schedules that were too ambitious, which delayed FAA certifications. The USAF can mitigate some of these concerns by increasing its institutional knowledge and familiarization of FAA certification processes, learning from prior CDA certification programs, anticipating friction points early, discussing potential points of friction with both FAA and the OEM, and ensuring regular and ongoing discussions between all the stakeholders so problems that arise can be managed early. Finally, modifications and requirements should be altered as little as possible during the certification process. Changes not included in the original design will delay or prevent aircraft from achieving FAA certification. That adds further difficulty to an already complex process and could force the USAF to treat the new design as a normal acquisition program.

Challenges Stemming from Test and Evaluation

The test and evaluation (T&E) process involves its own unique set of challenges in the CDA certification process, according to several T&E experts we spoke with—and was a topic not raised in other aspects of our research.[43] The T&E process for CDA is often considered to be an afterthought rather than an integral component of successful FAA certification. For a CDA program, there will likely be hundreds of test plans, including engineering flight plans owned by the OEM and certification flight test plans owned by the government. One SME noted that from a CDA perspective, it is difficult to make an assessment of what will work because the program is simultaneously in the process of developing test plans and certifying the aircraft. Rather than

---

[42] EASA SME, interview with the authors, May 31, 2022.

[43] T&E SMEs, interview with the authors, June 28, 2022.

developing test plans prior to certification, these two activities are happening at the same time, which does not allow for benefits to be derived from the normal T&E process.

The SMEs also noted that for CDA programs they were most familiar with, the OEM had an exceptional amount of responsibility for the T&E process, often to the point of having ownership over processes that were typically government led.[44] Unclear, or uncommon, authorities that give ownership of additional T&E processes to the vendor were discussed as adding confusion, extra work, and contributing to disagreements between the OEM and the government.

For example, because T&E authority resides with the OEM, it is possible for the OEM to initiate changes during the ongoing certification processes without fully understanding or considering the effects on all others involved. Decisions such as adding new subcontractors to the development of the CDA could require development of new test plans to address new seams between components, or even reopen certification test plans that were already finalized and deemed complete. Furthermore, the USAF might not have the ability to push back on these OEM-driven decisions because the aircraft might not in fact be owned by the USAF at certain points in development; therefore, the USAF cannot dictate how to handle such situations. On the other hand, even if the CDA being tested and certified *is* a USAF asset, because the vendor typically leads the modifications and testing, disagreements can arise over such issues as which personnel will be involved (OEM or government) or which crew will be present in the flight deck. SMEs felt that setting the contract terms was a way to address some of the problems, such as limiting when and how changes with subcontractors can be made within the program so that the certification process is not delayed by late changes to T&E plans. The group of SMEs also felt that handing over the majority of test activities to the OEM was not the best way to conduct these activities.[45]

The SMEs also reiterated views held by other SMEs interviewed for this project that it is important to consider the type of aircraft to be used as a CDA for the military, including details of the mission it is intended to support and in what operating environment. Furthermore, they noted that it was important to include a testing team as early as possible to understand these factors and the implications for sustainment. If the program office wants to build a testing strategy at the same time as its sustainment strategy, it is especially important to include a testing team early in the program because of the multiple stakeholders involved.

The FAA is concerned with safety for its certification and the military is focused on utility for its mission. Involving T&E personnel in the discussion addresses the gap that is left from FAA certification, which is not concerned with executing the military mission well. Critical testing for the mission could be missed if T&E is not considered. Because the typical

---

[44] This relationship reminded at least one SME of the Total System Performance Responsibility contracts used in the 1990s and 2000s, and widely considered by the group of SMEs to be a failed acquisition approach that had lasting negative effects on acquisition within the USAF.

[45] One SME noted that it is important to outline the Master Test Plan correctly and recalled examples of successful test teams he knew of as ones that had been mixed with both the OEM and government personnel.

stakeholders for civil certification are the OEM and the FAA, the program office relies on those entities to do their part, and T&E is even further removed from the conversation. According to the SMEs, it is critical to understand the mission and for T&E personnel to be involved as early as possible or the mission of the aircraft gets lost in the certification activities.

To support a program office in involving T&E professionals early, outlining appropriate T&E responsibilities with the OEM, and understanding the intended mission of the CDA, T&E offices have representatives in each directorate for a CDA. The AFLCMC's Acquisition Center of Excellence also maintains a repository of lessons learned to help new start programs.[46] To capitalize on these lessons learned, an important action for the near term would be for CDA program offices to consult AFLCMC to take action to mitigate some of these T&E concerns.

Conclusions and Recommendations

In this chapter, we discussed the FAA's certification process, the impetus for the USAF's pursuit of FAA certification of military CDA, and the benefits and challenges to that process. In this final section, we highlight key findings and associated recommendations.

1. Early, open, and regular communication between all parties can help DAF scope CDA projects and become aware of any issues throughout the process. The FAA MCO's SMEs are eager to be used as a resource to help program offices inform DAF decisions.

    a. **Recommendation:** The USAF should play a larger role in defining the relationship between all the parties in the certification process. This starts with setting realistic internal expectations of what the certification process can provide for the USAF. It also means a better understanding of what FAA certification provides, the OEM's role and potential challenges, and insisting on being involved in regular discussions.

2. Knowledge and education of certification processes do not appear standardized. This could contribute to confusion or unrealistic expectations of partners. Gaining more insight into the FAA certification process could help USAF personnel better describe the intended functions of military systems to be installed on CDA and better manage programs in general, smoothing the process. Expert knowledge of the process appears to be diffuse within AFLCMC, held by individuals who are consulted but might not be involved in every CDA program.

    a. **Recommendation:** Develop and foster in-house talent for certification and CDA management, for example:
        i. Career field education and training plans could be developed for CDA programs, perhaps an AFSC for enlisted personnel who can specialize in the field or a special experience identifier (SEI) to denote experience with CDA acquisition.
        ii. An aircraft certification service/flight standards service training program that embeds USAF personnel in the FAA also could be developed.

---

[46] T&E SME, interview with the authors, June 28, 2022.

iii.   Program offices should develop skills to better self-govern compliance with FAA requirements.

3. When considering the platform's mission and modifications from the base design, understand that more modifications could complicate the process.

   a. **Recommendation:** Consultations with the FAA MCO before a CDA acquisition decision is made can help the USAF decide on the best course of action (COA) and refine requirements. Likewise, for sustainment, the USAF will need to consider strategies early in the process to take full advantage of the potential benefits of certification. This includes discussions with the FAA about MTI approvals for maintenance and sustainment of the CDA fleet.

Chapter 3. Sustainment Implications and Strategies for CDA

Given the relatively large proportion of weapon system life cycle costs attributable to operating and support (O&S) costs, the USAF should consider various acquisition strategies to reduce O&S costs to the greatest extent possible.[47] Aside from the acquisition benefits of CDA, such as the avoidance of lengthy and costly development efforts and reduced procurement costs by taking advantage of learning and rate effects associated with existing commercial platforms, the USAF might also realize sustainment cost benefits. Some of the key sustainment benefits of CDA come from the potential to leverage existing infrastructure supporting the commercial platform and from economies of scale pricing for parts shared with the commercial variant. However, some of these potential benefits might be challenging to fully realize because of DoD- and USAF-specific regulations and differences between the operating environments of the commercial variant and the CDA.

In this chapter, we first discuss some of the potential sustainment benefits that the USAF might realize with the procurement of CDA. Included in this discussion are some of the challenges that the USAF might encounter that could inhibit its ability to realize these benefits and ways to maximize benefits. Second, we enumerate several sustainment risks that the USAF might encounter and mitigation strategies to deal with each of the potential risks. Third, we discuss several factors that could influence the type of sustainment strategy that a given program might wish to pursue, whether it be primarily organic, CLS, or a mixture of these two broad strategies. Finally, we offer recommendations that the USAF should consider for future CDA acquisitions.

Sustainment Benefits of CDA Acquisition and Realization Challenges

The sustainment benefits associated with CDA are affected by the timing of the CDA procurement relative to the overall production life cycle of the commercial platform. In the case of the KC-46A, the USAF sought procurement relatively late; Boeing continues to produce 767-400 freighters but not passenger versions. Some benefits are maximized when the CDA procurement occurs early in the production life cycle of the platform while others are maximized when the CDA procurement occurs later in the production life cycle. To help illustrate this, Figure 3.1 provides a notional example where CDA procurement occurs relatively late in commercial variants operational life cycle, similar to the KC-46A scenario.

---

[47] See Gary Jones, Edward White, Erin T. Ryan, and Jonathan D. Ritschel, "Investigation into the Ratio of Operating and Support Costs to Life-Cycle Costs for DoD Weapon Systems," *Defense Acquisition Research Journal*, Vol. 21, No. 1, 2014, pp. 441–462.

Figure 3.1. Operational Life Cycle of Fleet

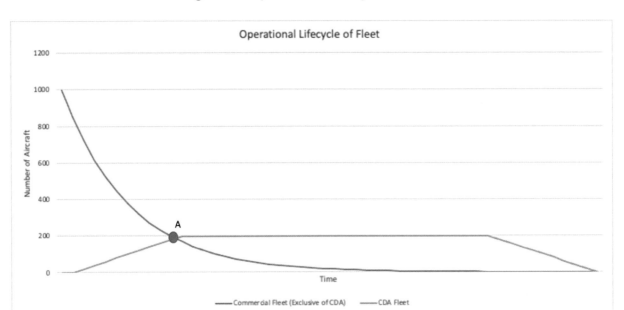

The blue line depicts a notional commercial fleet's operational life cycle over time while the orange line shows the procurement and operational life of a CDA based on the same platform as the commercial platform. As demonstrated in this notional example, which is similar to the KC-46A scenario, the commercially operated fleet is dwindling rapidly as the CDA procurement begins. At point A in the figure, the CDA variant becomes the majority operator among the total global fleet. This depiction can help elucidate some of the benefits and forgone benefits from procuring late in the life cycle of the overall aircraft's procurement. The usefulness of understanding where CDA procurement occurs in the platform production and operational life cycle is that many sustainment benefits associated with CDA occur when CDA resources can be shared with other operators of the fleet.[48] When operators of the platform are no longer operated by other entities, the benefits of shared resources will likely be reduced or eliminated altogether.

Although the focus of this chapter is the sustainment implications and strategies associated with CDA, understanding where the CDA is procured in the platform life cycle introduces trade-offs with procurement and sustainment costs and benefits. Although many sustainment benefits are maximized when procurement occurs earlier in the life cycle and the overlap between CDA and commercial operations is longest, procurement pricing will likely be lower when CDA are purchased later in the life cycle and learning and rate effects are incorporated into pricing.[49] This latter scenario likely would have been the case with the KC-46A. That said, there are some sustainment benefits from later procurements, which will be discussed in this chapter.

---

[48] Stockman et al., 2011, pp. 61–63.

[49] Stockman et al., 2011, p. 41.

CDA offers potential sustainment benefits that are well documented in several studies, reports, and white papers. However, it can still be difficult for the USAF to fully realize those benefits. Table 3.1 summarizes some of those benefits and challenges as well as enablers that the USAF should consider to realize these potential benefits. These benefits are discussed in the sections that follow.

Table 3.1. CDA Sustainment Benefits

Expected CDA Sustainment Benefits	Challenges Realizing Benefit	Considerations for Maximizing Benefits
Parts pool sharing	• Level of modification • DoD repair facilities are not FAA Part 145 certified	• Limit modification • Obtain and maintain same airworthiness requirements for parts
Pool of new and used parts from retiring commercial fleet	• Realization depends on platform life cycle and timing of fleet retirement	• Consider trade-offs of early and late buys in commercial life cycle
Existing commercial infrastructure, inventory, and supply chain systems	• "Core" and 50/50 statutory requirements	• Consider CLS options
Continuously evolving technology driven by commercial market	• Modification can make integration with upgrades difficult and costly	• Limit modification to decrease integration and testing
MSG-III procedures	• Limited experience using commercial technical materials and maintenance procedures	• Invest resources in expertise and training in commercial maintenance practices and procedures
Sustaining engineering maturity and RMA knowledge	• Benefits affected by difference in commercial and military missions	• Understand how differences affect prior knowledge and data
Leverage third-party parts and repairs for potential cost savings	• Requires parts and repairs certified by the FAA to be airworthy and interchangeable with OEM parts and repairs	• More likely with CLS sustainment • Invest resources to properly train and hire AF engineers to support third-party part and repair source approval
Potential warranties offered on commercial products	• Managing warranties with many suppliers • Could affect ability to obtain technical data	• Consider warranties with initial procurement pricing • Understand impact on ability to obtain technical data

NOTE: AF = Air Force; MSG-III = Maintenance Steering Group-III; RMA = reliability, maintainability, availability.

Parts Sharing and Access to New and Used Parts from Retiring Fleets

Parts pooling, the first benefit in Table 3.1, is maximized when the CDA platform is also operated by other entities (e.g., commercial fleets). Sharing parts with other operators is one of the most cited sustainment benefits of CDA.[50] Unsurprisingly, this benefit is realized only when there are other operators of the shared platform, and the benefit would likely shrink as the fleet size of commercial operators of the platform shrink. Considering the example of the 767, allies are expected to operate the 767 until approximately 2048, with small commercial fleets retiring well before that. Therefore, in the case of the KC-46A, the benefits of shared parts and parts pooling benefits might not be as lengthy or as large as it might have been if the commercial platform was relatively early in its production life cycle. By 2048, the KC-46A is projected to be an orphan fleet and will presumably no longer be able to realize parts pooling benefits.[51]

Although the ability to share parts with a large commercial fleet might no longer exist, there are potential benefits that can be realized when a CDA becomes the sole operator. As commercial fleets retire, an excess of used aircraft, used parts, and even new parts no longer needed for retiring aircraft, will be available to the remaining CDA fleet.[52] Therefore, this introduces a bit of a trade-off associated with the timing of CDA procurement in the platform life cycle from a parts perspective. Early buys can maximize the overlap of commercial operations with USAF operations and the ability to leverage the economies of scale benefits of shared parts with commercial operators. Later buys can enable the orphan CDA fleet to be the sole beneficiary of available parts remaining in the market. However, the latter benefit is likely smaller because parts manufacturers will likely be planning accordingly for retiring fleets and the remaining pool of parts might not be a significant benefit.

Despite the often cited benefit of parts pooling, the USAF might not be able to maximize this benefit because of its inability to participate in two-way sharing.[53] Currently, DoD does not have the authority to repair parts and place them in the pool for non-DoD operators to use. Commercial operators can use only parts repaired in an FAA Part 145 certified repair facility, and DoD repair facilities are currently not Part 145 certified.[54] Therefore, if a part is repaired in a USAF repair facility, that part must remain in the USAF supply chain and cannot be put back in the parts pool shared by commercial operators, which limits the economies of scale benefits for DoD operators of CDA. The economies of scale benefits are smaller for DoD operators as a larger portion of their parts will come from their internal supply chain of parts that are repaired in-house and not shareable with the larger pool. Parts that fail and need repairing more often on CDA relative to their commercial counterpart could result in a suboptimal quantity in their supply chain and less ability to maximize the purchase of parts from the shared pool. With that said, a cost-benefit analysis would be required to determine whether the benefits are worth the

---

[50] Stockman et al., 2011, pp. 61, 67; and USAF, 2009, p. 83.

[51] An *orphan fleet* refers to a CDA that no longer has a shared operational commercial equivalent fleet.

[52] Stockman et al., 2011, p. 61.

[53] Stockman et al., 2011, p. 65.

[54] This point was noted in interviews with various FAA SMEs and the KC-46 sustainment office.

cost of certifying facilities to participate fully in two-way sharing and supply refurbished parts for commercial operator use.

The amount of modification or deviation from the green aircraft is an additional factor in determining the ability to benefit from parts pooling.[55] The more that the CDA deviates from the commercial variant and its associated unique parts, the smaller the number of shared parts with the commercial fleet becomes, and therefore, the potential use of parts pooling is also reduced.

Given the noted challenges associated with maximizing realization of parts pooling benefits, the USAF should consider several things when attempting to quantify this potential benefit. First, consider the trade-offs associated with early and late buys in any potential platform's production and operational life cycle. Second, obtaining and maintaining the same FAA certification as commercial operators will maximize the USAF's ability to leverage parts shared with commercial operators.[56] Finally, limiting modification of the commercial variant will maximize the percentage of shared parts with the commercial variant and therefore the potential cost savings from parts pooling.

Other Shared Resources with the Commercial Fleet

The third benefit, leveraging existing commercial infrastructure, inventory, and supply chains, is also affected by the operational overlap of the USAF CDA and the commercially operated fleets.[57] Once the USAF becomes the sole operator, it would become solely responsible for the commercial infrastructure, inventory, and supply chains if they were being leveraged by the USAF. Therefore, the USAF would no longer be able to leverage these resources at a shared, and presumably lower, cost. In addition to the monetary benefits of leveraging existing physical and operational infrastructure, many of the commercial operators maintain worldwide maintenance sites, which could benefit the operational readiness of USAF fleets operating anywhere with hangers, parts, and maintainers available across the globe.[58] Realization of these benefits would require special arrangements with commercial operators, but nonetheless, it is a potential benefit of CDA.

Although these are potential benefits of CDA, statutory requirements (e.g., "core," source of repair, and the 50/50 rule) can require a significant amount of organic maintenance and limit the ability to leverage commercial infrastructure and contractor supply chains. That said, if an acquisition is unconstrained by statutory requirements for organic maintenance, considering CLS

---

[55] The *green* aircraft refers to the unmodified variant of the aircraft.

[56] USAF, 2009, p. 69.

[57] USAF, 2009, p. 83 and Defense Science Board, *Buying Commercial: Gaining the Cost/Schedule Benefits for Defense Systems*, Office of the Under Secretary of Defense for Acquisition, Technology, and Logistics, February 2009, p. xv.

[58] Stockman et al., 2011, p. 41.

options using existing infrastructure and supply chains could be a viable cost saving strategy to consider.

Commercially Driven Technology Upgrades

The commercial market imparts significant pressure that is driven by competition to improve existing aircraft and their maintenance procedures. These upgrades can improve both the performance and safety of the platform and include such things as new, advanced materials and manufacturing techniques; upgrades to aircraft software; and optimized maintenance procedures. As a result of these competitive pressures in the commercial market, the USAF benefits from these upgrades with the procurement of a CDA. These upgrades can affect the sustainment of CDA in several ways. One of the most common upgrades in modern aircraft is the software. These updates can be particularly challenging for CDA if there is tightly coupled mission-specific software integrated with the green aircraft's software. Software maintenance can become costly if continual upgrades require mission-specific software to be modified to properly integrate with green upgrades. Time will tell if this becomes a problem for the KC-46A.

Another specific maintenance change that might prove to be beneficial is the USAF needs to consider how commercial practices driven by MSG-III could affect maintenance procedures. MSG-III changes can hasten improvements to maintenance procedures and technical manuals.[59] However, the USAF has limited experience in using commercial technical materials and maintenance procedures, which might result in challenges leveraging and adapting to commercial manuals. To realize MSG-III benefits to the greatest extent, the USAF should invest resources in expertise and training in commercial maintenance practices and procedures.

CDA Sustainment Leverages Mature Platforms

One of the key benefits of procuring CDA, particularly those using platforms with many flying hours, is that the CDA benefits from a mature and tested platform.[60] This enables the USAF to avoid some of the early challenges in a development program, such as problem resolution and associated schedule slips. Furthermore, maintenance practices could be optimized based on the high operational tempo of commercial operators. Again, depending on how long the platform has been operated in the commercial sector, there might be extensive RMA data to inform and optimize sustainment and preventative maintenance decisions.[61]

As with many of the other benefits discussed, the advantages associated with leveraging existing platforms is dependent on when the CDA is procured in the platform life cycle. In the case of the KC-46A, where 767s have been operating for many years, major platform problems

[59] Stockman et al., 2011, p. 64.

[60] Stockman, et al., 2011, pp. 63–64.

[61] Stockman, et al., 2011, pp. 63–64.

should be resolved and optimal sustainment schedules should be well established. However, if a CDA is procured early in a platform's life cycle, the USAF might share some of the challenges associated with the development of a new platform. Furthermore, extensive RMA data won't be available, which could lead to some uncertainty in optimal maintenance schedules and aircraft availability.[62]

Although the benefits noted are real, the mature platform and RMA data associated with many flying hours as a commercial variant might not be completely applicable because of the mission differences between commercial operators and the military. Although commercial aircraft often have flying hours far exceeding military aircraft, the missions and associated stressors on the aircraft are quite different. Military aircraft such as the KC-46A are used in harsh environments, pushed to their operational limits, and often used in training exercises requiring more-fatiguing takeoffs and landings. All of these factors can influence the usefulness of commercial RMA data and affect maintenance schedules.

Potential Cost Savings from Use of Third-Party Parts and Repairs

Another potential benefit that has been studied is the use of third-party parts and repairs to reduce costs. Parts Manufacturer Approval (PMA) parts and Designated Engineering Representative (DER) repairs are provided by third-party companies and are certified by the FAA to be airworthy and are interchangeable with parts or repairs from the OEMs. Some evidence suggests that there could be large cost savings by using PMA parts and DER repairs. The history of their use within the USAF on various CDA has been mixed.[63] Sustainment contracts for the commercial derivative KC-10 airframe and engine gives broad latitude in using PMA parts and DER repairs whereas the KC-135 makes little use of these strategies.[64]

Historically, commercial airlines foster cooperative relationships with the supply base by sharing part usage and failure data with potential suppliers whereas the USAF rarely pursues similar relationships. Furthermore, commercial airlines consider PMA parts and DER repairs regardless of whether they own the technical data rights; the USAF usually considers these alternatives only for parts for which they own technical data. PMA part and DER repair contractors can negotiate their own data rights with part OEMs, thus making it unnecessary for the USAF to spend large amounts of money for its own data rights.

By procuring CDA, an opportunity exists to reduce sustainment costs by using third-party parts and repairs but the benefit is likely limited to cases in which the USAF primarily uses CLS

---

[62] Stockman, et al., 2011, pp. 63–64.

[63] Mary E. Chenoweth, Michael Boito, Shawn McKay, and Rianne Laureijs, *Applying Best Practices to Military Commercial-Derivative Aircraft Engine Sustainment: Assessment of Using Parts Manufacturer Approval (PMA) Parts and Designated Engineering Representative (DER) Repairs*, RAND Corporation, RR-1020/1-OSD, 2016.

[64] Chenoweth et al., 2016, p. 73.

sustainment. Furthermore, the use of PMA and DER requires that the USAF has engineers who are properly trained to support PMA and DER source approval.

Warranties Are Commonly Offered with Commercial Products

A final benefit and consideration that any buyer of a commercial product should consider are any warranties associated with the product.[65] This is also true of CDA. One of the difficulties associated with realizing this benefit is that the management of warranties can be quite burdensome, given the number of suppliers involved in the manufacturing of modern aircraft such as the KC-46A.[66] Additionally, if warranties are offered in the product, then manufacturers are less willing to provide technical data rights for the product and this information can be critical, particularly if there is a requirement or desire to maintain the CDA organically.[67] Therefore, warranties should be a critical factor in the procurement pricing of CDA while considering the implications and cost of acquiring necessary technical data.

Sustainment Risk Factors for CDA and Potential Mitigation Strategies

The USAF should be aware of several sustainment-related risks when procuring CDA. These risks are summarized in Table 3.2 along with potential risk mitigation strategies for each one. Many of the risks noted in this section have a relation to the benefits discussed previously in this chapter. For instance, some of the challenges to realizing the potential CDA sustainment benefits could become risks once the USAF opts to pursue a CDA acquisition. Therefore, the reader might note some recurring themes in this section from the earlier discussion on sustainment benefits. Some of this overlap is summarized in the overarching conclusions at the end of this chapter.

CDA Outliving Commercial Variant Introduces Risks

The first risk in Table 3.2 is related to the critical decision regarding timing of CDA procurement in the production life cycle of the commercial variant and how this affects the life cycle of the CDA relative to the commercial fleet. It is not uncommon for the USAF to sustain their fleets for much longer than their commercial counterparts; therefore, CDAs almost always outlive their commercial variant counterparts.[68] Furthermore, if the USAF procures late in the commercial variant's production life cycle, then the USAF could be operating an orphan fleet for many years.[69] Operating an orphan fleet introduces some sustainment risks to the USAF,

---

[65] Defense Science Board, 2009, p. xv; and USAF, 2009, p. 56.

[66] USAF, 2009, p. 81.

[67] USAF, 2009, p. 81.

[68] USAF, 2009, p. 79.

[69] Stockman et al., 2011, p. 21.

particularly when it comes to long-term support from the OEM. Some of these potential risks include parts obsolescence and diminishing manufacturing sources.[70] The potential for these risks causing real issues is largely dependent on the OEM's business case for maintaining manufacturing capability for a relatively small fleet of aircraft as the commercial fleet retires. As a mitigating effort, it is crucial that the USAF continually monitor the commercial market and global fleets retirement plans to understand when and what impacts the dwindling commercial fleet could have on the CDA's sustainment efforts. The USAF will need to plan for becoming the sole operator of the platform, such as the KC-46A, and address issues such as parts obsolescence to ensure uninterrupted operations.

Additionally, as the USAF becomes the primary or sole operator of a platform, it in essence becomes the de facto manager of that platform's supply chain and sustaining engineering efforts.[71] Again, these changes will require careful planning, particularly if the USAF relies on CLS for these sustainment functions. A plan for the potential need to transition to organic supply chains and sustaining engineering will need to be considered. This might require significant costs for technical data rights that could be avoided by using CLS sustainment.

Table 3.2. CDA Sustainment Risk Factors and Mitigation Strategies

Sustainment Risk Factors Associated with CDA	Risk Mitigation Strategies
1. CDA is likely to outlive commercial counterpart which could affect long-term support	• Monitor the commercial market to understand when the USAF might become the sole operator and plan for long-term impacts
2. Government might become de facto manager of platform supply chain and sustaining engineering if they become the sole operator	• If using CLS, consider a plan for transitioning to organic supply chains and sustaining engineering
3. Lack of technical data and software can lock the USAF into less-than-optimal or costly sustainment arrangements	• Understand where CDA might be in the product support life cycle and the amount of modification to determine what data rights are needed and when
4. Subsystem technical data might not be available to the OEM, which would require separate negotiations with subcontractors	• Have a clear understanding early on of who owns technical data rights for various parts
5. Commercial variants of CDA are often updated, which would require DoD to plan for obsolescence and technology refresh	• Ensure close communication with OEM to understand future technology upgrades and their implications for the sustaining engineering of CDA
6. CDA user is usually forced to rely on OEM software management, accepting changes to the software as they occur throughout the life of the system	• Plan for software changes and understand the implications for integration with mission-specific software and systems

---

[70] USAF, 2009, p. 20.

[71] USAF, 2009, p. 89.

Sustainment Risk Factors Associated with CDA	Risk Mitigation Strategies
7. More deviation from green aircraft results in less ability to leverage commercial sustainment resources	• Carefully analyze and reduce modifications to the absolute minimum to maximize the ability to leverage commercial sustainment resources
8. Integration of mission-specific sensors and related software with green aircraft software could result in increased costs	• Plan for the activities and costs associated with commercial-driven software changes and their impacts to integrated mission software and systems
9. FAA certification requires maintenance and training to be done IAW FAA procedures instead of DoD procedures	• Invest in research and expertise associated with commercial maintenance procedures

Technical Data Rights Can Present Significant Risk to the USAF

One of the most cited risks associated with procuring commercial items is the difficulty in obtaining technical data rights from the manufacturer. Although it is not surprising that manufacturers are reluctant to give these rights to a customer who is not an investor in the development because IP rights are valuable assets, the inability for the USAF to obtain certain technical data or software can impede its ability to maintain products organically.[72] Furthermore, lacking technical data can lock the USAF into suboptimal and costly sustainment arrangements preventing organic or open competition for CLS maintenance.[73] A further risk related to technical data is that the prime contractor might not own subsystem technical data, creating the need for separate negotiations with several vendors or suppliers.[74] As noted in the supplemental report on the KC-46A, more than 800 subcontractors worked on KC-46A components for Boeing.[75]

To mitigate some of these risks, the USAF should understand where CDA might be in the product support life cycle and the amount of planned modification to determine what data rights are needed and when. One suggestion is for the USAF to include, as a part of the contract with the OEM's "data assertion list," where the OEM and/or modification contractor defines the available data so that the government could assert which data it needs access to and when.[76] Such a document is typically a living document that is updated as circumstances and needs change. To mitigate the risk associated with having to negotiate with many potential suppliers, the USAF should have a clear understanding early on of who owns technical data rights for various parts and if specific rights with the multitude of suppliers are attainable if necessary. Finally, if technical data rights are unattainable or too costly, using third-party contractors for PMA parts or DER repairs might be an option to avoid OEM lock-in and to reduce cost. Oftentimes, PMA

---

[72] USAF, 2009, p. 92.

[73] USAF, 2009, p. 79.

[74] USAF, 2009, p. 86.

[75] Sacks, Younossi, and Clayton, 2023, p. 7.

[76] Stockman et al., 2011, p. 74.

manufacturers and DER repairers will have negotiated their own data rights with the OEMs, thus eliminating the USAF's need to obtain data rights in some circumstances.[77]

Upgrades to Green Variant Can Cause Downstream Sustainment Risks

Risks associated with upgrades and technology refresh to the commercial, or green, variant have effects on CDA. As we discussed earlier, commercial market competition drives continuous improvement to the commercial variants. Although these upgrades are a benefit to the USAF because they can take advantage of these benefits in their CDA version, there are also inherent risks. The USAF must plan for these updates, obsolescence, and technology refresh.[78] Mitigating these risks requires close communication with the OEM to understand the future landscape of technology upgrades driven by the commercial market and the implications for sustaining engineering of the CDA.

Technology updates are especially common with the operating software on the aircraft. In fact, many CDA rely on the OEM to manage and maintain software updates, accepting software updates as they occur throughout the life of the system.[79] Mitigating any risks associated with unanticipated software updates requires close communications between the OEM and whoever is managing software maintenance to understand the implications for integration with mission-specific software.

Heavily Modified CDA Increase Sustainment Risk

Unsurprisingly, as the CDA becomes more heavily modified and the deviation from the green aircraft increases, program risks also increase. One of those risks is that there will be less ability for the USAF to leverage shared sustainment resources with the commercial variant, therefore reducing some of the promises of cost savings associated with CDAs. As discussed in the prior section, this includes reduced ability to share parts and existing infrastructure. To mitigate these risks, the USAF should carefully analyze and minimize modifications to the greatest extent possible to increase their ability to avoid CDA specific investments and leverage existing commercial resources for sustainment.

A related issue to modifications is the extent to which mission specific sensors and software are integrated with the green aircraft, such as the Remote Vision System installed on the KC-46A. As the green aircraft makes updates to the platform and its software, there could be costly impacts on the mission-specific applications requiring additional sustaining engineering, integration, and testing.[80] The USAF should plan accordingly to understand the potential cost

---

[77] Chenoweth et al., 2016, p. 36.

[78] USAF, 2009, p. 86.

[79] USAF, 2009, p. 80.

[80] USAF, 2009.

and mission impacts associated with downstream impacts of green aircraft modifications to mission-specific hardware and software.

New and Unfamiliar Commercial Maintenance Procedures Driven by FAA Certification Requirements

Finally, the preference to obtain and maintain FAA certification for CDA, and the benefits this certification provides, introduces some risks because maintenance procedures required to maintain FAA certification are less familiar to the USAF. Anytime an organization adopts new procedures, there is a learning curve that must be accounted for, as well as associated impacts to schedule and cost. As an example, to maintain the KC-46A organically and maintain FAA certification, the USAF has adapted its maintenance procedures to align more closely with commercial procedures using more-frequent but shorter duration maintenance checks versus the commonly used five-year programmed depot maintenance event. The KC-46A has required the depot facilities to achieve the MTI designation of an FAA facility to maintain FAA certification of the CDA. This type of requirement is something that the USAF will need to consider with future CDA acquisitions where organic maintenance is the sustainment strategy. To mitigate the risks associated with learning and adapting to new maintenance procedures, the USAF should invest in research and expertise in this area.

Factors Influencing Sustainment Strategies for CDA

Several factors can influence whether organic or CLS depot maintenance makes sense for CDA. Table 3.3 summarizes some of these factors and how each factor influences the sustainment strategy. Although some of these factors are true not just for CDA but also military-developed aircraft, we discuss how CDA are particularly influenced, where applicable. It should be noted that almost every aircraft in the USAF fleet is sustained via a mix of sustainment strategies, including both CLS and organic maintenance. Oftentimes, the mix of strategies is broken down along the various sustainment work streams (e.g., program management, product support integration, sustaining engineering, supply chain management, and depot maintenance). Again, this is true of both CDA and military developed aircraft. So, although aircraft might be discussed as being organically sustained or sustained via CLS as a primary strategy, there are almost always portions of the overall strategy using both organic maintenance and CLS.

Table 3.3. Factors Influencing Sustainment Strategy

Factors Influencing Sustainment Strategy	Influence on Sustainment Strategy for CDA
Fleet size	• Small fleets favor CLS arrangements because of large investment costs for depot activation that might not be justified for small number of aircraft
Available depot capacity	• Retiring aircraft might offer opportunity to leverage available capacity and use organic maintenance in cost-effective manner • Unavailable depot capacity might make CLS sustainment strategies more affordable
Depot capabilities	• USAF facilities and maintainers might lack equipment and expertise to adequately sustain CDA and future upgrades, making CLS sustainment a more viable option
Commercial platform life cycle stage	• Commercial platforms closer to retirement make organic support more viable as sole operator of fleet with sustainment extending well beyond commercial variant
Ability to obtain technical data rights and/or software code	• Rights to technical data and software code can favor CLS sustainment when costs of rights are prohibitive
Core requirement	• Core requirement mandates the USAF to maintain an organic capability
50/50 statute	• The USAF must meet statute requiring at least 50 percent of sustainment activities funded using organic capability

One of the most obvious influences on the decision to use organic or CLS sustainment is the projected fleet size for a given program. The USAF has several CDA fleets that consist of relatively small quantities (e.g., C-37B, E-4B, VC-25, C-40), and these fleets are mostly maintained via CLS contracts. Small fleets usually do not justify the large investments in depot activation, including depot facilities, support equipment, and maintainer expertise for a small number of aircraft. Therefore, the USAF sustains these fleets mostly via CLS.

The second key factor in determining whether a CDA should be maintained organically is the available depot capacity. For instance, a retiring platform might free up capacity (both physical capacity and labor) in existing depots, making organic maintenance a cost-effective option for the USAF. As an example, the retiring KC-135 is gradually opening capacity for the USAF to perform organic maintenance on the KC-46A. Despite this logical use of available capacity from retiring aircraft, existing facilities might require significant modifications because of differences in the outgoing and incoming platforms—the KC-46A, for instance, is larger than the KC-135 it is replacing. In cases where depot capacity is limited, product support business cases should address whether the costly investments in new depots make sense and whether CLS options might be more cost effective.

In addition to capacity, the USAF should consider whether existing depot capabilities can accommodate new, more technologically advanced aircraft in an affordable way. Again, any product support business case should address the costs associated with investing in the necessary capabilities for a new aircraft and whether the optimal decision is to invest in the capability and provide the support organically or rely on CLS options. If the USAF facilities and maintainers lack equipment and expertise to adequately sustain CDA and future upgrades, this might make CLS sustainment more viable.

As discussed earlier in the report, the USAF often maintains aircraft much longer than their commercial equivalents. Less overlap in commercial and CDA operations might make organic sustainment more viable because some of the sustainment benefits from shared operations are not realized. Therefore, CDA acquisitions of commercial aircraft closer to retirement might be better off using organic strategies from the start to avoid a potentially costly transition from CLS to organic and to reap organic sustainment benefits such as greater control and flexibility for surge capacity scenarios.

Another key factor influencing the sustainment strategy is the USAF's ability to obtain technical data rights and/or the software code for a specific platform. This includes both the willingness of the OEM and multitude of suppliers to provide such data and the potential cost if the data owner is willing to provide it. Technical data and software code can be critical and are often necessary if the USAF wishes to maintain the CDA organically. If the OEM or owner of data is unwilling to provide necessary data or if it is cost prohibitive to acquire, the USAF might need to rely on CLS sustainment. This could prove difficult for the KC-46A because the USAF has declared it to be a core asset requiring organic-oriented maintenance to meet the service's 50/50 rule, discussed in detail below.

The final two factors are in some ways the most important because they are binding, statutory requirements that can require a significant portion of sustainment to be performed using organic means.[81] First, if a certain acquisition is determined to be a core requirement, then by default it must be primarily maintained using organic maintenance. Core requirements require the USAF to maintain an organic capability to have maximum flexibility over sustainment and in-house capability to meet mission demands without relying on contractor support. The second statute is the 50/50 requirement that DoD imposes, requiring each service's budget to include a minimum of 50 percent organic maintenance across all weapon systems being maintained. Fortunately, small fleet sizes will not have a significant impact on 50/50 calculation and therefore can largely use CLS sustainment. But particularly large acquisitions (e.g., KC-46A) might require a large portion of organic maintenance if otherwise large CLS contracts would result in a violation of

---

[81] Although the statutory requirements are not specific to CDA, they require mention because all other factors become much less important if the platform is determined to be "Core" and if there are 50/50 constraints the AF must consider. For a discussion on the various statutes affecting the use of CLS sustainment, see Michael Boito, Cynthia R. Cook, and John C. Graser, *Contractor Logistics Support in the U.S. Air Force*, RAND Corporation, MG-779-AF, 2009, pp. 10–15.

the 50/50 requirement. In conclusion, if a new acquisition is determined to be core or there are real pressures imposed on the USAF's ability to abide by the 50/50 requirement for a new acquisition, then these statutes can force the USAF into a sustainment strategy that is primarily organic, even if the strategy is suboptimal. However, given the constraints posed by core and 50/50 requirements, the upside of maintaining a minimum organic capability provides a minimum in-house enterprise sustainment capability that can be particularly useful as reach back for orphaned CDA dealing with issues such as parts obsolescence.

Consider Trade-Offs When Choosing a Sustainment Strategy

Choosing between CLS and organic strategies for sustainment introduces trade-offs, some of which are unique to CDA aircraft. Figure 3.2 depicts three of these trade-offs.

Figure 3.2. CDA Sustainment Strategy Trade-Offs

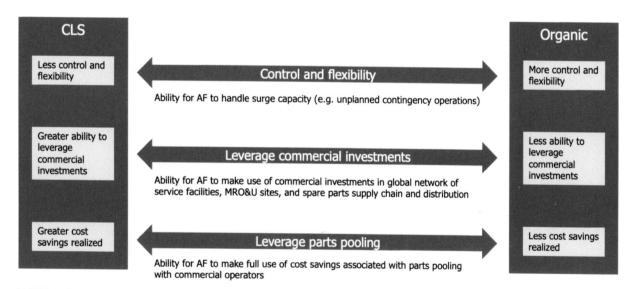

NOTE: AF = Air Force; MRO&U = Maintenance, Repair, Overhaul, and Upgrade.

The first trade-off is not unique to CDA, but it is important to note because it can be of critical importance for meeting mission needs. The benefits of organic depots, namely more control, flexibility, and ability to handle surge capacity based on USAF needs (e.g., unplanned contingency operations), might outweigh some of the opportunity costs associated with organic maintenance of CDA. Some interviews and studies have also suggested that CLS is more expensive than organic but there is mixed data supporting this claim and it is highly dependent on several program specific circumstances.

One trade-off favoring the use of CLS revolves around the ability to leverage commercial investments. By using organic strategies, the USAF would forgo maximizing the ability to leverage such investments. There is an inherent opportunity cost with organic maintenance by not leveraging an established commercial service and global network of service facilities, maintenance, repair, overhaul, and upgrade sites, and spare parts distribution that has already been invested in by commercial operators. As a related point, we found that the potential exists to leverage commercial operators for heavy maintenance. This type of strategy would be an example of leveraging commercial investments and potentially realizing cost savings from those investments. Although we were unable to discuss specifics with the Navy's P-8A program office, the P-8A is a Boeing 737 derivative that is primarily CLS-maintained via both OEM and third-party providers. Through an arrangement with Boeing, the P-8A leverages a commercial operator, Delta TechOps, to provide some level of airframe and engine maintenance.[82] It might be in the USAF's interest to understand some of the benefits and challenges that the Navy has experienced with this type of sustainment arrangement.

Finally, as with leveraging commercial investment, parts pooling cannot be fully maximized using organic maintenance because USAF repair facilities are not FAA Part 145 certified. CLS arrangements create more opportunity to realize cost savings from parts pools as CLS maintenance and parts repairs might be conducted in FAA-certified repair facilities enabling two-way parts exchange.

Cost Comparisons Between Sustainment Strategies for CDA Are Inconclusive

Although some studies have compared CLS and organic maintenance costs by reviewing product support business case analyses (PS-BCAs) to make comparisons, a limited number of such business cases for CDA-specific aircraft were available that allowed us to draw many conclusions. Furthermore, one of the most relevant to review, the KC-46 PS-BCA, did not assess CLS options for depot maintenance because it had already been determined to be core, thus making an organic capability mandatory. We did note, however, that in the limited number of CDA PS-BCAs we examined, analogies to legacy systems were used that in some cases were not CDAs. Therefore, accounting for potential CDA benefits (e.g., parts pooling) in cost comparisons would not be accounted for. The USAF should try to collect more data and attempt to better understand quantitatively the potential sustainment cost savings associated with cited CDA sustainment benefits. Using this information, adjustments can be made, or sensitivity analysis can be performed in PS-BCAs to attempt to quantify benefits such as parts pool sharing and leveraging commercial investments in sustainment activities.

Organic Depot Maintenance Challenges Can Be Exacerbated with CDA Acquisitions

Regardless of the acquisition type, whether CDA or military developed, standing up organic depots can be challenging. However, these challenges can be exacerbated with CDA acquisitions. The acquisition of CDAs usually allow a program to forgo Milestone A and begin the acquisition process at Milestone B or Milestone C, leaving less time to plan for and

---

[82] "Delta Air Lines: Partners with Boeing, U.S. Navy to Provide Maintenance on P-8A Poseidon Aircraft," *Market Screener*, November 7, 2018.

potentially secure military construction funding for new or repurposed depots. It can be difficult to secure military construction funds early enough because depot requirements (e.g., the size of hangars) driven by specific platform characteristics need to be decided before Congress will allocate those funds. As a risk reduction, it can be beneficial for the initial contract with a contractor to stipulate that, despite a plan for organic maintenance, the OEM would provide depot support in the case where USAF depots would not be activated in time for the first round of C-Checks.[83] This strategy was pursued by the KC-46A program office. However, because of a slip in the delivery of the aircraft, the USAF was able to organically perform the first scheduled C-Checks.

Conclusions and Recommendations

Several key aspects of CDA can have significant impacts on the potential benefits of CDA acquisition from a sustainment perspective. As discussed in this chapter, although the benefits and risks are numerous, a few key factors are central to sustainment concerns and lead to several recommendations for the USAF.

- The commercial production and operational life cycle of potential CDA options are critical in understanding potential sustainment benefits and the extent to which the USAF can realize CDA sustainment benefits. Maximizing the overlap of CDA operations with commercial variants maximizes benefits such as shared parts, infrastructure, and supply chains. Furthermore, once the commercial variant retires, risks such as parts obsolescence and diminishing manufacturing sources can require mitigation efforts.

  - **Recommendation:** Invest time and resources in understanding the commercial variant's life cycle prior to acquisition and during acquisition to ensure that CDA benefits are maximized and risks are avoided. This knowledge is also key in being able to plan for any necessary transitions from CLS to organic sustainment once the CDA becomes an orphan fleet.

- Limiting modification maximizes the sustainment benefits of a CDA acquisition in several ways. Heavily modified aircraft reduce the ability to share parts and other existing infrastructures. In addition, greater modification increases schedule and cost risks because of more integration and sustaining engineering efforts. Any future upgrades to the green variant can have ripple effects with integrated modifications requiring re-engineering, integration, and testing.

  - **Recommendation:** During acquisition, carefully consider the necessary level of modification required to meet mission objectives and make efforts to minimize modifications when possible if pursuing CDA is the preferred strategy. If a significant

---

[83] A *C check* is a specific level of maintenance that historically is used in the commercial maintenance sector and adopted by the KC-46. Checks range from A to D with A and B checks considered line or light maintenance and C and D checks categorized as base or heavy maintenance. The time interval and resource requirements increase with each higher level check.

amount of modification is needed to meet a system's defined requirements, CDA benefits will be limited.

- Continually monitor commercial best practices for sustainment and investigate strategies used in the commercial market, including increased use of PMA parts and DER repairs and using commercial airlines for heavy maintenance.

  - **Recommendation:** Invest in research and expertise related to the sustainment of CDA, including expertise in MSG-III maintenance practices and procedures and other commercial best practices.

- Although there are many theoretical sustainment benefits cited in existing literature, there is a lack of empirical data demonstrating to what extent the USAF has realized sustainment benefits from a CDA acquisition. This is understandable; it is always difficult to quantify benefits when a counterfactual is not observed.[84] Nonetheless, this lack of empirical knowledge makes it difficult to make data-driven decisions.

  - **Recommendation:** Invest in data collection and research to better quantify the potential sustainment benefits of CDA. This empirical data would improve PS-BCAs and therefore enable the USAF to make more-informed decisions on whether a CDA for a specific acquisition offers the best value from a sustainment perspective.

---

[84] For instance, although parts cost data is probably easily obtainable for a given CDA, understanding the cost of the same parts had the aircraft not been a CDA and benefited from the economies of scale of parts pooling would be difficult to quantify.

Chapter 4. The Application of Digital Engineering in CDA Acquisition

The U.S. military services are increasingly using DE to improve the performance of the DoD acquisition and sustainment enterprise.[85] Although systems engineering firms have been using more-sophisticated forms of DE to help develop systems for many years, the services are now trying to leverage complementary data, models, tools, and infrastructure to better meet their own goals—including lowering costs, better meeting schedules, and better defining and achieving capability requirements. As the USAF focuses on keeping pace with the near-peer threat, DE has been identified as the "key to unleashing the speed and agility we need to field capability at the tempo required to win in a future conflict with a peer competitor."[86]

Establishing the use of DE in the USAF is an incomplete process, with ongoing pilot programs that extensively employ DE to apparent success thus far (including the Next-Generation Air Dominance fighter and Sentinel intercontinental ballistic missile) and the gradual increase in use of DE activities across many more conventional program offices.[87] However, there are substantial challenges to the broader application of DE that must be overcome—perhaps most significantly in terms of the competency of the government workforce in digital tools, DE processes, and software development, but also in terms of data availability and the immaturity of tools and information technology (IT) infrastructure, among other challenges.[88]

---

[85] DoD defines *digital engineering* as "[a]n integrated digital approach that uses authoritative sources of systems' data and models as a continuum across disciplines to support lifecycle activities from concept through disposal." See DoD, *Digital Engineering Strategy*, Office of the Deputy Assistant Secretary of Defense for Systems Engineering, June 2018; and Defense Acquisition University, "DAU Glossary of Defense Acquisition Acronyms and Terms," webpage, undated-a.

[86] Darlene J. Costello, "Guidance for e-Program Designation," memorandum for the acquisition enterprise, U.S. Department of Defense, May 3, 2021.

[87] Tom McDermott, Paul Collopy, Chris Paredis, and Molly Nadolski, *Enterprise System-of-Systems Model, Digital-Engineering Transformation: Summary Report of SERC Technical Report*, Stevens Institute of Technology, Systems Engineering Research Center, SERC-2018-TR-109, November 20, 2018; John A. Tirpak, "Roper's NGAD Bombshell," *Air & Space Forces Magazine*, October 1, 2020; Patrick Tucker, "The Virtual Tools That Built the Air Force's New Fighter Prototype," *Defense One*, September 15, 2020; Frank Wolfe, "AF Chief: Digital Engineering 'Key Aspect' of NGAD," *Defense Daily*, September 22, 2020; and Shaun Waterman, "GBSD Using Digital Twinning at Every Stage of the Program Lifecycle," *Air & Space Forces Magazine*, April 8, 2022.

[88] Sean Robson, Bonnie L. Triezenberg, Samantha E. DiNicola, Lindsey Polley, John S. Davis II, and Maria C. Lytell, *Software Acquisition Workforce Initiative for the Department of Defense: Initial Competency Development and Preparation for Validation*, RAND Corporation, RR-3145-OSD, 2020; Kirsten M. Keller, Maria C. Lytell, and Shreyas Bharadwaj, *Personnel Needs for Department of the Air Force Digital Talent: A Case Study of Software Factories*, RAND Corporation, RR-A550-1, 2022; David R. Graham, Gregory A. Davis, Cheryl D. Green, Peter K. Levine, Maggie X. Li, and David M. Tate, *An Assessment of Options for Strengthening DoD's Digital Engineering Workforce (Revised)*, Institute for Defense Analyses, IDA Paper P-21560 (Revised), February 2022; and Bill

Therefore, it is critical to understand how, where, and when DE should be employed given the limited digital resources that the USAF has at its disposal today.

This chapter concerns the use of DE within the context of CDA. We build upon past RAND work on DE to consider the unique nature of CDA acquisitions, present findings on what characteristics of CDA acquisitions resist the successful application of DE, and make recommendations on how planning can mitigate those difficulties. Although DoD and the DAF have been focused in recent years on growing the use of DE within the acquisition enterprise, published policies, guidance, and resources are not tailored to CDA programs.[89] Therefore, it is important to consider the CDA characteristics when planning for DE in a CDA program. In contrast to FAA certification and contractor-support sustainment (the other two acquisition tools examined closely in this research effort), DE is generally made more problematic for CDA acquisitions because of difficulties in procuring data rights, shortened development time frames, fixed design of the commercial platform, and a leaner acquisition workforce.

Planning for Digital Engineering

Crafting an acquisition strategy is just as critical for CDA acquisition as conventional military development programs and potentially includes planning how to use DE within a given CDA program.[90] DE-derived benefits are built upon a foundation of investments, enablers, and specific activities. Figure 4.1 contains a general framework showing the relationship between a desired benefit derived from DE and supporting DE activities, enablers, and investments.

Nichols, "Challenges in Making the Transition to Digital Engineering," *Software Engineering Institute Blog*, Carnegie Mellon University, December 13, 2021.

[89] The digital engineering webpage from the Under Secretary of Defense for Research and Engineering includes a roundup of the primary DE resources from DoD. See Office of the Under Secretary of Defense for Research and Engineering, "Digital Engineering," webpage, undated.

[90] USAF, 2009.

Figure 4.1. General Framework for Planning from DE-Derived Benefit to DE investments

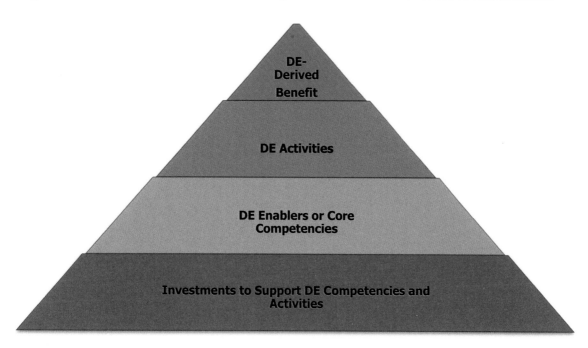

Although investments come first when executing a program and DE efforts, planning DE efforts must start with an identification of the desired DE goals and working from there to identify activities, enablers, and investments. The order of planning and the order of execution are opposite. The investments required, such as in workforce or digital infrastructure, would depend on the desired DE-derived benefit and activities planned but, in many cases, need to be implemented well before an organization expects to realize the benefits of DE.

Figure 4.2 shows an example of how a benefit (namely, more timely and efficient sustainment) drives specific activities, enablers, and investments. This example is not intended to present detailed planning for this DE objective (it is too high level and generic for that) but to instead clarify the types of enablers and investments to which we are referring. In this illustrative example, predictive maintenance and organic sustainment engineering are examples of DE activities to achieve the goal of more timely and efficient sustainment.[91] DE enablers (which could also be called core competencies) such as data rights, digital infrastructure, and workforce competency are required to support those DE activities. Required investments, made earlier in the life cycle, to create and support those enablers include workforce hiring and training, purchasing IP, and model development, among others.

---

[91] Predictive maintenance and organic sustainment engineering are quite broad categories that could be applied differently in different programs and may be more or less reliant on DE tools and techniques. Here, we refer to examples of these activities that do depend on DE, for example, organic sustainment engineering that uses model-based systems engineering (MBSE) or a digital authoritative source of truth.

Figure 4.2. Example Planning Framework from DE-Derived Benefit to DE investments

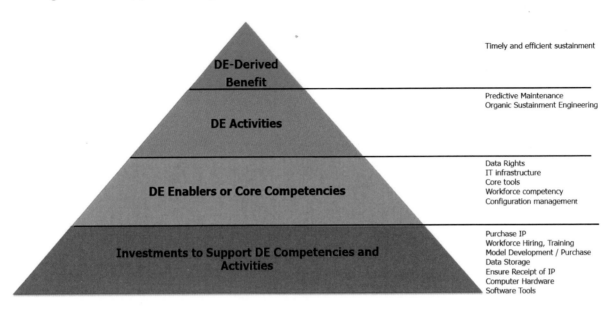

Pursuing a significant DE effort should start with early planning that focuses on the goals of the program that DE would support. As in many other aspects of managing an acquisition program, early decisions, actions, or lack of action might control the freedom that the program office has throughout the life cycle. This approach is like the often-given guidance that programs must plan for life cycle sustainment up front.[92]

These investments will be made not only by the program office but also by the government enterprise, contractors, and even operational community—which complicates planning for DE efforts. Table 4.1 expands the illustrative example from Figure 4.2 and aligns the elements against these four groups of stakeholders. As the figure indicates, investments and activities must be synchronized and coordinated across the acquisition enterprise if many DE efforts are to be successful.

---

[92] See Defense Science Board, 2009, for an example.

Table 4.1. Example Mapping of DE Investments Across Stakeholders

Stakeholder	Investments	Enablers	Benefits
Operational community	• User feedback opportunities • Embedded operators	• Governance and policy • Workforce competency	• Timely sustainment
Government enterprise	• Hiring appropriate engineers • Workforce training • Cloud storage	• Data rights • Workforce competency • Governance and policy	• Cost-efficient sustainment • Timely sustainment
Government program office	• Model development • Purchase IP • Ensure receipt of IP • Software tools • Workforce training	• Data rights • Workforce competency • Configuration management • Core tools	• Cost-efficient sustainment
Contractor/developer	• Model development • Software tools • Workforce training	• Workforce competency • IT infrastructure • Core tools	• Better performance

To summarize, our work has stressed the importance of early planning as part of crafting an acquisition strategy, starting from the identification of program goals that could be supported by DE. That planning will drive what activities, enablers, and investments are required to successfully apply DE tools and techniques. Without that early planning and investment, the program could lack the options to insert certain DE activities later in the life cycle without enormous difficulty.

Digital Engineering in CDA Acquisitions

Although every CDA acquisition is different, they have common characteristics, generally benefits from leveraging the commercial platform, that are particularly true for CDAs that are more similar to the commercial platform. These characteristics, although they might be good for the program overall, can make implementation of DE more difficult. As a result of less modification of the CDA platform, the following aspects could be affected:

- **Schedule:** might result in faster schedule and less time to make required CDA investments
- **IP:** might result in more difficulty or expenses to acquire required IP and data rights
- **Workforce:** might result in leaner acquisition workforce that could challenge DE efforts
- **Budgets:** might result in lower budgets that could constrain DE efforts
- **Design flexibility:** might result in fewer areas or systems where DE can be applied.

CDA acquisitions are intended to leverage the past investment, design work, and known reliability of commercially developed aircraft platforms. One goal of a CDA acquisition strategy is shorter schedules and lower costs relative to a newly developed military aircraft.[93] For CDA programs that are closer in design to the CDA aircraft, you might expect cost savings to be maximized and schedule to be minimized.[94]

Our interviewees expressed concern that CDA acquisitions make it even more difficult for the government to obtain technical data rights, and the recent example of legal battles on KC-46A IP, leading Boeing and the USAF to litigation, has highlighted those concerns.[95] Without access to technical design information, many engineering techniques, digital or otherwise, are not possible.[96]

Because engineering companies—including the usual military aerospace prime contractors—have been employing some types of DE (such as MBSE and related earlier precedents or computer-aided design) for many years, some of the DE benefits early in the life cycle might already be built into the CDA acquisition program.[97] On the other hand, some parts of the design (whether components, subsystems, or the entire platform) are already set and there is no flexibility in the design. Because many of the design choices have already been established, there might be fewer opportunities to apply DE to the developmental phases of the life cycle (e.g., smaller materiel design space or fewer components to be designed).[98] Therefore, the developmental benefits of DE might be reduced for CDA acquisitions.[99]

---

[93] Because some of the system development was completed as part of designing the commercial platform, CDA acquisitions are typically expected to compress the schedule before Milestone B (assuming the CDA acquisition program is successful). See USAF, 2009; Stockman et al., 2011; and Defense Science Board, 2009.

[94] Stockman et al., 2011.

[95] In many cases, OEMs make much of their profits on military aircraft by supporting the sustainment of those aircraft, rather in the original purchase. This disincentivizes them from selling IP without charging very high costs for those data rights, especially for commercially developed platforms. Daniel Seiden, "Boeing Opposes Air Force's Demand for Tanker Aircraft Drawings," Bloomberg Law, January 20, 2022.

[96] Camm, Carter, et al., 2021.

[97] *MBSE* is defined as "the formalized application of modeling to support system requirements, design, analysis, verification and validation activities beginning in the conceptual design phase and continuing throughout development and later lifecycle phases" (International Council on Systems Engineering, *Systems Engineering Vision 2020*, INCOSE-TP-2004-004-02, September 2007, p. 15). MBSE traces its lineage from pioneering software engineering work in the 1980s that focused on visually and mathematically modeling the interdependencies of complex systems, through an explosion of computer-aided engineering tools in the 1990s, and consolidation into the standardized Unified Modeling Language, which was then largely replaced as the standard tool by a variant called Systems Modeling Language in 2003. An increasing DoD focus on joint and multinational operations in the 1990s led to the initial application of architecture frameworks to weapon systems, which were then formalized as the DoD Architectural Framework in 2003.

[98] As we discuss throughout this report, increasingly departing from the design of the commercial aircraft platform typically reduces the benefits of using a CDA.

[99] This is particularly concerning because the developmental benefits of DE are the mostly extensively demonstrated benefits compared with potential benefits later in the life cycle (e.g., more-timely sustainment) or inherently governmental benefits (e.g., refinement of capability requirements or better prediction of cost or schedule).

These factors make it critical to assess the feasibility of a DE plan. Constraints such as workforce, schedule, budget, and IP, among others, could render a DE plan unactionable or not worth the required investment.

Decisionmaking for Digital Engineering in CDA Acquisitions

Figure 4.3 gives a high-level overview of the decisionmaking framework or decision model that we believe will support careful evaluation of whether to pursue a DE effort in a CDA program. It is a structured process intended to incorporate assessment of the issues discussed earlier in this chapter.

Figure 4.3. High-Level Decision Process for Planning DE in a CDA Acquisition

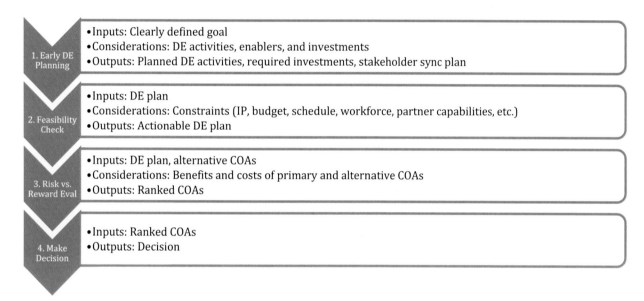

First, early DE planning maps a clearly defined programmatic goal to require DE competencies and investments (which we discussed previously in this chapter using the example of timely and efficient sustainment). Early planning results in a well-defined DE plan, including activities and investments that are synchronized among stakeholders.

Second, given the unique complications that CDA programs might impose on DE efforts, such as relatively expensive data rights and shortened development schedule, it is critical to assess the feasibility of that DE plan. By evaluating the various constraints against the requirements of successfully applying DE tools and techniques, a determination that a DE plan is actionable should be made.

Third, this DE plan should be compared with alternative COAs. Conducting such business case analyses is a common part of crafting an acquisition strategy and is not limited to the CDA or DE contexts. But in the case of CDA programs, the application of DE early in the life cycle might be particularly challenging, and these developmental benefits have the most precedents.

Although such analysis is not unique to CDA programs or DE, there are unique aspects when planning for DE in CDA programs that need to be considered.

This process should result in a well-defined DE plan that is actionable and has been evaluated against alternative acquisition strategies. If a plan is the most beneficial, despite the unique challenges that CDA programs will face when using DE, then the decision should be made to pursue it.

Findings and Recommendations on Digital Engineering

We summarize our primary findings and corresponding recommendations on the use of DE in CDA acquisitions in Table 4.2. The expected benefits of a successful CDA program could make the use of DE more difficult, but these risks could be mitigated through early systems engineering and planning efforts.

Table 4.2. Findings and Recommendations on Digital Engineering in CDA Acquisitions

Findings	Recommendations
Development-related benefits of DE could be reduced (or already in design of commercial platform) for CDA acquisitions	• Consider feasibility of applying DE techniques and tools to subsystems undergoing military modification
Designing from a commercial aircraft platform, particularly with little modification, could make implementing DE more difficult	• Realistically consider all constraints, particularly ones stemming from the nature of CDA acquisitions • Compare benefits and costs against alternative strategy options (DE and non-DE based) to ensure that DE is an appropriate and optimal strategy to achieve program goals
Successfully realizing DE benefits will require early systems engineering efforts to identify required enablers and investments	• Begin planning DE efforts when forming an acquisition strategy • Begin planning process by considering priority goals of the program and matching to promising DE activities • Apply systems engineering methods to identify DE activities, enablers, and investments required for success • Apply decision aid (see Figure 4.3) to support the decision on whether to pursue a given DE effort
Investments typically span stakeholders and efforts must be synchronized and coordinated to be successful	• Consider equities, responsibilities, and capabilities of partners and stakeholders during planning and decision to pursue a given DE effort
Existing DoD DE policy and guidance does not specifically address CDA acquisitions	• Be wary of following DoD policy and guidance on DE without considering unique characteristics of a CDA acquisition

Chapter 5. Conclusions and Recommendations

In this report, we have identified benefits and challenges associated with the acquisition and sustainment of CDA programs. We have outlined lessons learned in three specific areas of acquisition and sustainment: the role of FAA certification within the CDA process, possible sustainment arrangements that could be the most beneficial to CDA, and the application of DE practices in CDA acquisition. Many of these recommendations enable effective approaches to technical data rights management. More detail on this topic can be found in the appendix.

Future CDA programs could consider the recommendations summarized here to improve the process of CDA acquisition and sustainment.

General Considerations

- Establish a center of expertise for CDA acquisition that could be accessed by all program offices.
- Standardize contract clauses and provisions to minimize rework and reduce source selection time.
- Establish a market research office to share insights into industry experiences and regulatory changes.
- Collaborate with Navy CDA programs to share lessons learned.
- Develop training opportunities for acquisition professionals that are focused on unique features of CDA acquisition.
- Embed USAF employees into FAA to gain experience with and exposure to FAA regulations and processes.
- Colocate members of the program office with the prime contractor to better integrate the government into the IPT.
- Increase communication with the operating command and bases to monitor requirements development and operational performance.
- Partner with airline or aircraft brokers to better understand their contracts (e.g., performance, guarantees, warranties, services).
- Identify the appropriate level of expertise in critical acquisition areas.
- Include lawyers and contract experts during contract development and negotiations.
- Recognize that the potential systems integration and sustainment costs far outweigh the initial acquisition costs of aircraft.
- Many of the decisions made early in the acquisition process will limit the ability to adapt later in the aircraft life cycle.
- Address sustainment specifics during contracting phase.
- Engage sustainment experts during contract negotiations.
- Identify and leverage commercial standards in all areas of acquisition, including modular open systems architecture where possible.

FAA Certification Recommendations

- Early, open, and regular communication between all parties can help the DAF scope CDA projects and become aware of any issues throughout the process. The FAA MCO is eager to be used as a resource to help program offices and inform DAF decisions. The USAF should play a larger role in defining the relationship between all the parties in the certification process. This starts with setting realistic internal expectations of what the certification process can provide for the USAF. It also means better understanding of what FAA certification provides, the OEM's role and potential challenges, and being involved in regular discussions.
- Knowledge and education of certification processes does not appear standardized. This could contribute to confusion or unrealistic expectations of partners. Gaining more insight into the FAA certification process could help USAF personnel better describe the intended functions of military systems to be installed on CDA and better manage programs in general, which could smooth the process. Expert knowledge of the process appears to be diffuse within the AFLCMC and is held by individuals who are consulted but might not be involved in every CDA program. The USAF should develop and foster in-house talent for certification and CDA management. For example, it could do the following:
  - develop career field education and training plans for CDA programs, and perhaps establish an Air Force Specialty Code for enlisted personnel who can specialize in the field, or an SEI to denote experience with CDA acquisition
  - establish an aircraft certification service/flight standards service training program that embeds USAF personnel in the FAA
  - develop program offices skills to better self-govern compliance with FAA requirements.
- When considering the platform's mission and modifications from the base design, understand that more modifications could complicate the process. Consultations with the FAA MCO before a CDA acquisition decision is made can help the USAF decide on the best COA and refine requirements. For sustainment, the USAF will need to consider strategies early in the process to take full advantage of the potential benefits of certification. This includes discussions with the FAA about MTI approvals for maintenance and sustainment of the CDA fleet.

Sustainment Recommendations

Several key aspects of CDA can have a significant impact on realizing potential benefits of CDA acquisition from a sustainment perspective. Although the benefits and risks are numerous, a few key factors are central to sustainment concerns and lead to several recommendations for the USAF:

- The commercial production and operational life cycle of potential CDA options are critical in understanding potential sustainment benefits and the extent to which the USAF can realize CDA sustainment benefits. Maximizing the overlap of CDA operations with commercial variants maximizes benefits such as shared parts, infrastructure, and supply chains. Furthermore, once the commercial variant retires, risks such as parts obsolescence and diminishing manufacturing sources can require mitigation efforts. Investing time and resources in understanding the commercial variant life cycle prior to and during acquisition could ensure that CDA benefits are maximized and risks are avoided. This knowledge is also key in being able to plan for any necessary transitions from CLS to organic sustainment once the CDA becomes an orphan fleet.

- Limiting modification maximizes the sustainment benefits of a CDA acquisition in several ways. Heavily modified aircraft reduce the ability to share parts and other existing infrastructures. In addition, greater modification increases schedule and cost risks because of more integration and sustaining engineering efforts. Future upgrades to a green variant can have ripple effects with integrated modifications requiring re-engineering, integration, and testing. During requirements development, the USAF should carefully consider the necessary level of modification required to meet mission objectives and make efforts to minimize modifications when possible if pursuing CDA is the preferred strategy.

- Continually monitor commercial best practices for sustainment and investigate strategies used in the commercial market, including increased use of manufacturer approved parts and DLR repairs and using commercial airlines for heavy maintenance. Invest in research and expertise related to the sustainment of CDA including expertise in MSG-III maintenance practices and procedures and other commercial best practices.

- Although many theoretical sustainment benefits are cited in existing literature, there is a lack of empirical data demonstrating to what extent the USAF has realized sustainment benefits from a CDA acquisition. This is understandable because it is always difficult to quantify benefits when a counterfactual is not observed.[100] Nonetheless, this lack of empirical knowledge creates difficulty in making data-driven decisions. Investing in data collection and research could better quantify the potential sustainment benefits of CDA. These empirical data would improve PS-BCAs and therefore enable the USAF to make more-informed decisions on whether a CDA for a specific acquisition offers the best value from a sustainment perspective.

Digital Engineering Recommendations

Because the baseline commercial aircraft have already benefited from DE principles by design, development-related benefits of DE could be reduced for CDA acquisitions. However, programs should consider feasibility of applying DE techniques and tools to subsystems undergoing military modification, as shown in the following examples:

- Designing from a commercial aircraft platform, particularly with little modification, could make implementing DE more difficult. Realistically, programs should consider all the constraints, particularly ones stemming from the nature of CDA acquisitions—that is, compare benefits and costs against alternative strategy options to ensure that DE is an appropriate and optimal strategy to achieve program goals.

---

[100] For instance, although parts cost data is probably easily obtainable for a given CDA, understanding the cost of the same parts had the aircraft not been a CDA (and benefited from the economies of scale of parts pooling) would be difficult to quantify.

- Successfully realizing DE benefits will require early systems engineering efforts to identify required DE enablers and investments. This starts with planning DE efforts when forming an acquisition strategy. Programs should begin the planning process by considering priority goals of the program and matching those goals to promising DE activities. Furthermore, programs should apply systems engineering methods to identify DE activities, enablers, and investments required for success.
- Investments typically span stakeholders, and efforts must be synchronized and coordinated to be successful. Therefore, consider equities, responsibilities, and capabilities of partners and stakeholders during planning and decision process when pursuing a DE effort.
- Existing DoD DE policy and guidance does not specifically address CDA acquisitions; therefore, DoD policy and guidance needs to be tailored for unique characteristics of a CDA acquisition.

Appendix. Technical Data Rights

Any time the government uses a vendor with a product that it sells on the commercial market, the topic of technical data rights inevitably becomes an important factor. Starting even prior to contract award and through the end of life of the product/program, technical data rights implications are woven throughout the program development and relationship between the government and vendor. Having access to the appropriate level and amount of data rights is often a critical element of a program because getting these elements right can have a positive impact on the government's ability to be more flexible in the planning, development, and sustainment of the product. Industry understands the implications of having technical rights to data, as their profitability is often tied to being able to sell a unique, proprietary technology. Conversely, the government has not always had the same kind of incentive to understand the nuances of technical data rights as well as industry does, and a program can be affected negatively. For this study, technical data rights for CDA components are directly related to certification efforts, DE, and sustainment options. As we previously observed, data rights have been the source of friction between the government and OEMs, which indicates there is an opportunity for data rights implications to be better understood for the benefit of future CDA and USAF weapons systems programs.[101]

RAND has conducted prior research in looking at data rights, particularly in the context of USAF weapon systems. Two studies published in 2021, *Managing Intellectual Property Relevant to Operating and Sustaining Major U.S. Air Force Weapon Systems* and *Data Rights Relevant to Weapon Systems in Air Force Special Operations Command,* have relevant information about data rights that can be extrapolated to understand implications for this current study on acquisition of CDA.[102] This appendix draws heavily on those reports, with direct information and findings included here pertaining to CDA. The observations and recommendations within this appendix are those of the authors of the two reports mentioned above, each worth reviewing in more depth on their own as well. The findings from each report could provide some useful concepts for the USAF to think about in future CDA programs as it determines the appropriate type and amount of technical data it needs to execute such a program for the next several decades.

One of the findings evident in both reports was that government buyers—in this case, the USAF—have the most leverage at the beginning of the process, and (more specifically) during

---

[101] For more on the historical background of the KC-46 program see Sacks, Younossi, and Clayton, 2023.

[102] Camm, Carter, et al., 2021; and Frank Camm, Thomas C. Whitmore, Guy Weichenberg, Sheng Tao Li, Phillip Carter, Brian Dougherty, Kevin Nalette, Angelena Bohman, and Melissa Shostak, *Data Rights Relevant to Weapon Systems in Air Force Special Operations Command*, RAND Corporation, RR-4298-AF, 2021.

the engineering and manufacturing development (EMD) source selection. This is because of the possibility of negotiating different or acceptable terms with potential vendors before one is locked in, so there is still potential to maximize flexibility and more-favorable data rights terms for the USAF in the contract. Some specific ways to gain that flexibility can come from using other contracting methods, including contract options, other transaction authority, or incentivizing.

Another observation from the *Data Rights Relevant to Weapon Systems in Air Force Special Operations Command* report found that, to exercise its right to the data rights it is entitled to (and to effectively use the data), the USAF must have both the appropriate license for the technical data in question and actually possess the data it wants to use. However, there are a lot of nuances that are not so clear-cut. OMIT and FFF data, for example, fall under unlimited rights, which the government is entitled to, but the rights become more restricted as they move down through government purpose rights and limited rights, not only in terms of what the government is entitled to as a result of the funding used to develop the technology but also in what can then be shared by the government for activities related to CDA, such as third-party maintenance support, diagnostics, upgrades, service-life extension, procurement of additional systems/subsystems, and replacement of diminished sources.[103] Further entwined into the complication is the source of funding that was used to develop the technology, which corresponds to varying levels of data rights. The line of funding quickly becomes unclear when technologies are iterated on and incorporated into the development of other technologies using multiple funding sources.

As exemplified through the KC-46 program, although OMIT and FFF data fall under unlimited rights, there are competing interpretations by the government and OEM on what are considered OMIT data and FFF data in practice. This lack of consensus adds an additional challenge to the current data rights regime being used for CDA programs because it creates a barrier for the USAF in obtaining the necessary data it expects to receive with no established route around such a barrier. The USAF might have believed they were to receive rights to certain data, which influenced its planning for operation of the aircraft and establishing a sustainment plan only to find itself in a different environment in which the choices it made for these program considerations are now at odds.

Complicating things further, USAF program offices do not necessarily have personnel with the appropriate or necessary data right backgrounds to deal with these issues.[104] This is specifically the case when it comes to personnel with legal expertise of data rights or with the level of understanding that is required to make the distinction between data rights (what the USAF entitled to) and the deliverables that should be associated with those rights (which deliverable was outlined in the contract). When OEMs make assertions about data rights, this

---

[103] Defense Federal Acquisition Regulation Supplement 252.227-7013, Rights in Technical Data—Other Than Commercial Products and Commercial Services, April 27, 2023.

[104] Camm, Whitmore, et al., 2021.

often means that the USAF personnel are not prepared to challenge those assertions and have difficulty in countering those claims that the USAF believes to be incorrect.

An interesting observation from Camm, Whitmore, et al. was that OEM contractors will typically use lawyers from the outset and during data right conversations, whereas USAF programs do not have in-house counsel and do not typically consult with lawyers.[105] In this context, the report found that USAF program personnel often feel outmatched by contractor teams and cannot counter with technical or legal rationale for assertions about technical data rights by the OEM, assertions that could, in fact, be incorrect.[106] The lack of understanding of the nuances of technical data from a legal perspective, and the cultural aversion to bringing in legal expertise, ultimately creates a situation in which the OEM has the upper hand at all stages of data rights discussions and day-to-day interactions, and this inhibits USAF programs from being able to take full advantage of their rights.

With these four major observations from the two reports, there are also several recommendations that are appropriate to highlight here as worth considering when deciding on the USAF's approach regarding data rights in future CDA. One would be to consider using nontraditional approaches to new contracting for technical data. The emphasis here is on *new* contracts because new contracts have the greatest potential for change compared with legacy programs. Again, this is because USAF leverage is greatest at the point *before* the vendor is locked in, and it is very difficult to make changes to an existing contract to obtain additional technical data rights.[107]

One suggestion put forth by prior RAND research is to consider using contract options.[108] A possible contract option would include a clause to buy IP at a designated price in the future with that price negotiated during EMD source selection, when the USAF has negotiating power, *not* after the awarding of the contract. The contract could define the data in a contract data requirements list and the price that the USAF would agree to pay only if it decided to exercise that option. The benefit to be gained here necessitates that these actions are explored and leveraged, as appropriate, prior to contract award when the vendor has not yet been selected and the USAF still maintains enough leverage to negotiate the terms it desires. The USAF would not

---

[105] Camm, Whitmore, et al., 2021.

[106] Camm, Whitmore, et al., 2021.

[107] Because the USAF spends most of its funding on operation and sustainment of legacy programs, there might be a desire to impart change on the data rights related to these programs to gain near-term cost savings. However, legacy programs often have less room for flexibility in their contracts, having been developed potentially decades ago, and the programs are often held to a sole source and the USAF has less leverage. Conversely, new contracts allow for the opportunity to make decisions that will affect operation and sustainment of the program in the future, giving an opportunity to make data rights decisions now that could affect future funding for O&S of the program in development.

[108] Camm, Carter, et al., 2021; Camm, Whitmore, et al., 2021.

be locked into paying for something it might determine it does not want in the future, and the OEM is not giving up too much of its IP without a real need.

A prior RAND report also found that it was critical to understand the role of time when comparing costs and benefits of investing in IP.[109] The study found that many USAF leaders prefer not to pay in advance for benefits to be realized in the future because they often work with limited budgets for certain programs, they have other priorities that need funding and will yield quicker results, and they will not be around in the future when these long-lasting programs finally reach a return on investment. This is understandable considering that CDA programs have a lifetime spanning several decades, much longer than many of those leaders will be involved in these programs.[110] Culturally, there is no incentive to worry about an issue that could be hard to justify in the present or to make decisions that leaders will never observe the effect of, even if beneficial to the USAF at large. Yet, given the length of contracts and the life cycle of CDA programs, time is a critical factor for making those decisions that will be long-lasting and difficult to change.

For example, there is a greater amount of detailed information in the RAND reports about the ways to evaluate an appropriate discount rate for the purchase of technical data based on what the OEM could be losing if it gives up rights to that technical data to the USAF today, and what the USAF would be willing to pay today based on the expected monetary benefits of the technical data rights to be realized in the future.[111] Understanding how each part would use discount rates leaves room for understanding where there could be a mutually acceptable point in which there would be gains for each party. But again, it is important to work through such a COA during EMD source selection, when this strategy could be discussed with multiple vendors, potentially allowing these discussions to influence the USAF's choice.

One area that appears to be at the forefront of actions to take in the near term would be to clarify OMIT and FFF data and what those terms really mean. This could have implications for future O&S and could set a precedent for future programs to avoid a similar disagreement. Because this type of data can be shared directly by the USAF, the effects of a clarification on these terms could set the tone for additional COAs that the USAF could take depending on the specifics of the clarification. To negotiate the right types and amounts of technical data, the definition of those data must first be explicitly agreed upon by both parties so that there is a point from which to work.

Lastly, the USAF could consider expanding technical data rights education in training. Of course, not every airman should become a data rights expert but many should have a working knowledge of when and where to challenge OEM assertions about data rights that conflict with

---

[109] Camm, Carter, et al., 2021.

[110] For example, the KC-135 *Stratotanker* has provided aerial refueling for the Air Force for more than 60 years. See USAF, "KC-135 Stratotanker," webpage, undated.

[111] Camm, Carter, et al., 2021; Camm, Whitmore, et al., 2021.

what is in the contract and to take an appropriate COA to address other data rights they could face day to day. One way to support this could be by developing an IP cadre made up of USAF personnel who can educate program offices on the fundamentals of data rights, apply expertise across the different program offices, and step in to address data rights concerns when needed.[112] Airmen who are not sure how to address an OEM making assertions about data rights that they do not believe to be true would have somewhere to elevate the concern.

The persistent concern for how to negotiate for and fully use technical data rights to allow the government to maximize benefits is enabled by having the right type and amount of technical data (including options to use organic or other sustainment strategies). As long as the government continues to use CDA for government and military purposes, technical data rights will continue to have implications for executing the program in a way that benefits the OEM and allows the USAF to carry out its mission in the way it deems most appropriate. Prior RAND research has found that the government need not attempt to buy all the technical data available or make drastic changes to the types of CDA efforts it pursues.[113] Rather, the research has found that the USAF should take several things into consideration, including thinking about data rights as early as possible to allow for informed negotiations and options that would give the government more-favorable terms for data rights throughout the life cycle of the program. Approaching each CDA program with this in mind would allow the USAF to consider the individual elements of each CDA program to craft the appropriate data rights regime required for each program to be successful.

---

[112] Camm, Carter, et al., 2021.

[113] Camm, Carter, et al., 2021.

Abbreviations

AFLCMC/WL	Air Force Life Cycle Management Center/Mobility & Training Aircraft Directorate
AFSC	Air Force Sustainment Center
ATC	Amended Type Certification
CDA	commercial derivative aircraft
CLS	contractor logistics support
COA	course of action
CQC	Certification and Qualification Committee
DAF	Department of the Air Force
DE	digital engineering
DER	Designated Engineering Representative
DoD	U.S. Department of Defense
EASA	European Union Aviation Safety Agency
EMD	engineering and manufacturing development
FAA	Federal Aviation Administration
FFF	form, fit, or function
IAW	in accordance with
IOC	initial operational capability
IP	intellectual property
IPT	integrated product team
IT	information technology
MBSE	model-based system engineering
MCO	Military Certification Office
MSG-III	Maintenance Steering Group-III
MTC	military type certificate
MTI	meet the intent
O&S	operating and support
OCCAR	Organisation for Joint Armament Co-Operation
OEM	original equipment manufacturer
OMIT	operation, maintenance, installation, or training
PMA	Parts Manufacturer Approval
PS-BCA	product support business case analysis
RMA	reliability, maintainability, availability
SEI	special experience identifier
SME	subject-matter expert

STC	Supplemental Type Certification
T&E	test and evaluation
TAA	Technical Airworthiness Authority
TC	Type Certification
USAF	U.S. Air Force

References

Aerospace Industries Association, Aircraft Electronics Association, General Aviation Manufacturers Association, and Federal Aviation Administration, *The FAA and Industry Guide to Product Certification*, 3rd ed., May 2017.

Air Force Policy Directive 62-6, *USAF Airworthiness*, Department of the Air Force, January 16, 2019.

Air Force Instruction 62-601, *USAF Airworthiness*, Department of the Air Force, June 11, 2010.

Boito, Michael, Cynthia R. Cook, and John C. Graser, *Contractor Logistics Support in the U.S. Air Force*, RAND Corporation, MG-779-AF, 2009. As of June 5, 2023:
https://www.rand.org/pubs/monographs/MG779.html

Camm, Frank, Phillip Carter, Sheng Tao Li, and Melissa Shostak, *Managing Intellectual Property Relevant to Operating and Sustaining Major U.S. Air Force Weapon Systems*, RAND Corporation, RR-4252-AF, 2021. As of August 25, 2022:
https://www.rand.org/pubs/research_reports/RR4252.html

Camm, Frank, Thomas C. Whitmore, Guy Weichenberg, Sheng Tao Li, Phillip Carter, Brian Dougherty, Kevin Nalette, Angelena Bohman, and Melissa Shostak, *Data Rights Relevant to Weapon Systems in Air Force Special Operations Command*, RAND Corporation, RR-4298-AF, 2021. As of July 13, 2022:
https://www.rand.org/pubs/research_reports/RR4298.html

Chenoweth, Mary E., Michael Boito, Shawn McKay, and Rianne Laureijs, *Applying Best Practices to Military Commercial-Derivative Aircraft Engine Sustainment: Assessment of Using Parts Manufacturer Approval (PMA) Parts and Designated Engineering Representative (DER) Repairs*, RAND Corporation, RR-1020/1-OSD, 2016. As of June 5, 2023:
https://www.rand.org/pubs/research_reports/RR1020z1.html

Costello, Darlene J., "Guidance for e-Program Designation," memorandum for the acquisition enterprise, U.S. Department of Defense, May 3, 2021.

Defense Acquisition University, "DAU Glossary of Defense Acquisition Acronyms and Terms," webpage, undated-a. As of July 21, 2022:
https://www.dau.edu/glossary/Pages/Glossary.aspx

Defense Acquisition University, "Military Commercial Derivative Aircraft (MCDA) and Federal Aviation Administration (FAA) Approved Meet the Intent (MTI)," webpage, undated-b. As

of August 26, 2022:
https://www.dau.edu/acquipedia/pages/articledetails.aspx#!720

Defense Federal Acquisition Regulation Supplement 252.227-7013, Rights in Technical Data—Other Than Commercial Products and Commercial Services, April 27, 2023.

Defense Science Board, *Buying Commercial: Gaining the Cost/Schedule Benefits for Defense Systems*, Office of the Under Secretary of Defense for Acquisition, Technology, and Logistics, February 2009.

"Delta Air Lines: Partners with Boeing, U.S. Navy to Provide Maintenance on P-8A Poseidon Aircraft," *Market Screener*, November 7, 2018.

Department of the Air Force, "Risk Identification and Acceptance for Airworthiness Determinations," Headquarters Aeronautical Systems Center (AFMC), Wright-Patterson Air Force Base, Bulletin AWB-013A, June 29, 2011.

DoD—*See* U.S. Department of Defense.

EASA—*See* European Union Aviation Safety Agency.

European Union Aviation Safety Agency, "About EASA," webpage, undated. As of July 29, 2022:
https://www.easa.europa.eu/the-agency/faqs/about-easa

Federal Aviation Administration, "Mission," webpage, undated. As of August 2, 2022:
https://www.faa.gov/about/mission

Federal Aviation Administration, "Certification," webpage, June 17, 2022. As of July 19, 2022:
https://www.faa.gov/uas/advanced_operations/certification/

Federal Aviation Administration, "Airworthiness Certification," webpage, June 29, 2022. As of July 19, 2022:
https://www.faa.gov/aircraft/air_cert/airworthiness_certification

Federal Aviation Administration Order 8110.4C, *Type Certification*, Federal Aviation Administration, October 12, 2005, change 6, March 6, 2017.

Federal Aviation Administration Order 8110.101A, *Type Certification Procedures for Military Commercial Derivative Aircraft*, Federal Aviation Administration, February 25, 2015.

Graham, David R., Gregory A. Davis, Cheryl D. Green, Peter K. Levine, Maggie X. Li, and David M. Tate, *An Assessment of Options for Strengthening DoD's Digital Engineering Workforce (Revised)*, Institute for Defense Analyses, IDA Paper P-21560 (Revised), February 2022.

International Council on Systems Engineering, *Systems Engineering Vision 2020*, INCOSE-TP-2004-004-02, September 2007.

Jones, Gary, Edward White, Erin T. Ryan, and Jonathan D. Ritschel, "Investigation into the Ratio of Operating and Support Costs to Life-Cycle Costs for DoD Weapon Systems," *Defense Acquisition Research Journal*, Vol. 21, No. 1, 2014.

Keller, Kirsten M., Maria C. Lytell, and Shreyas Bharadwaj, *Personnel Needs for Department of the Air Force Digital Talent: A Case Study of Software Factories*, RAND Corporation, RR-A550-1, 2022. As of July 13, 2022:
https://www.rand.org/pubs/research_reports/RRA550-1.html

McDermott, Tom, Paul Collopy, Chris Paredis, and Molly Nadolski, *Enterprise System-of-Systems Model, Digital-Engineering Transformation: Summary Report of SERC Technical Report*, Stevens Institute of Technology, Systems Engineering Research Center, SERC-2018-TR-109, November 20, 2018.

Nichols, Bill, "Challenges in Making the Transition to Digital Engineering," *Software Engineering Institute Blog*, Carnegie Mellon University, December 13, 2021. As of July 21, 2022:
http://insights.sei.cmu.edu/blog/some-challenges-in-making-the-transition-to-digital-engineering/

Office of the Under Secretary of Defense for Research and Engineering, "Digital Engineering," webpage, undated. As of July 28, 2022:
https://ac.cto.mil/digital_engineering/

Robson, Sean, Bonnie L. Triezenberg, Samantha E. DiNicola, Lindsey Polley, John S. Davis II, and Maria C. Lytell, *Software Acquisition Workforce Initiative for the Department of Defense: Initial Competency Development and Preparation for Validation*, RAND Corporation, RR-3145-OSD, 2020. As of July 13, 2022:
https://www.rand.org/pubs/research_reports/RR3145.html

Sacks, Benjamin J., Obaid Younossi, and Brittany Clayton, *Improving Acquisition and Sustainment Outcomes for Military Commercial Derived Aircraft: The KC-46A Pegasus Experience*, RAND Corporation, RR-A1676-1, 2023.

Seiden, Daniel, "Boeing Opposes Air Force's Demand for Tanker Aircraft Drawings," Bloomberg Law, January 20, 2022.

Stockman, William, Milt Ross, Robert Bongiovi, and Greg Sparks, *Successful Integration of Commercial Systems: A Study of Commercial Derivative Systems*, PESystems, Inc., and Dayton Aerospace, Inc., 2011.

Tirpak, John A., "Roper's NGAD Bombshell," *Air & Space Forces Magazine*, October 1, 2020.

Tucker, Patrick, "The Virtual Tools That Built the Air Force's New Fighter Prototype," *Defense One*, September 15, 2020.

United States Air Force Airworthiness Bulletin (AWB)-360, *Commercial Derivative Aircraft Airworthiness*, Department of the Air Force, September 1, 2021.

USAF—*See* U.S. Air Force.

U.S. Air Force, "KC-135 Stratotanker," webpage, undated. As of July 29, 2022: https://www.af.mil/About-Us/Fact-Sheets/Display/Article/1529736/kc-135-stratotanker/

U.S. Air Force, *Commercial Derivative Aircraft (CDA) Acquisition Guide*, November 2009.

U.S. Code, Title 10, Armed Forces, Subtitle A, General Military Law, Part V, Acquisition, Subpart D, General Contracting Provisions, Chapter 275, Proprietary Contractor Data and Rights in Technical Data, Subchapter I, Rights in Technical Data, Section 3771, Rights in Technical Data: Regulations.

U.S. Code, Title 49, Transportation, Subtitle VII, Aviation Programs, Part A, Subpart III, Safety, Chapter 447, Safety Regulation, Section 44701, General Requirements.

U.S. Code, Title 49, Transportation, Subtitle VII, Aviation Programs, Part A, Subpart III, Safety, Chapter 447, Safety Regulation, Section 44704 (b), Supplemental Type Certificates.

U.S. Department of Defense, *Department of Defense Handbook: Airworthiness Certification Criteria*, MIL-HDBK-516C, December 12, 2014.

U.S. Department of Defense, *Digital Engineering Strategy*, Office of the Deputy Assistant Secretary of Defense for Systems Engineering, June 2018.

Van Atta, Richard, Royce Kneece, Michael Lippitz, and Christina Patterson, *Department of Defense Access to Intellectual Property for Weapons Systems Sustainment*, Institute for Defense Analyses, IDA Paper P-8266, May 2017.

Waterman, Shaun, "GBSD Using Digital Twinning at Every Stage of the Program Lifecycle," *Air & Space Forces Magazine*, April 8, 2022.

Wolfe, Frank, "AF Chief: Digital Engineering 'Key Aspect' of NGAD," *Defense Daily*, September 22, 2020.